THE RHETORIC
OF REMEDIATION

Pittsburgh Series in Composition, Literacy, and Culture

David Bartholomae and Jean Ferguson Carr, Editors

THE RHETORIC
OF REMEDIATION

NEGOTIATING

ENTITLEMENT

AND ACCESS

TO HIGHER

EDUCATION

JANE STANLEY

UNIVERSITY OF PITTSBURGH PRESS

Published by the University of Pittsburgh Press, Pittsburgh, Pa., 15260

Copyright © 2010, University of Pittsburgh Press

Manufactured in the United States of America

Printed on acid-free paper

10 9 8 7 6 5 4 3 2 1

Library of Congress Cataloging-in-Publication Data

Stanley, Jane, 1950–

The rhetoric of remediation : negotiating entitlement and access to higher education /
Jane Stanley.

p. cm. — (Pittsburgh series in composition, literacy, and culture)

Includes bibliographical references and index.

ISBN-13: 978-0-8229-4386-0 (cloth : alk. paper)

ISBN-10: 0-8229-4386-7 (cloth : alk. paper)

1. University of California (System)—Admission. 2. University of California (System)—
History. 3. College freshmen—Rating of—California. 4. English language—Remedial
teaching. 5. English language—Study and teaching (Higher) 6. Students with social
disabilities—Education—California. I. Title.

LD741.S83 2010

378.1'6109794—dc22   2009029726

TO ANN STANLEY THO

CONTENTS

ACKNOWLEDGMENTS

THE IDEA FOR this book arose from a series of conversations with UC Berkeley's Glynda Hull about the ways in which remediation might be reconceived in composition generally and at UC Berkeley specifically. This work is indebted to those conversations. An observation that David Bartholomae made helped the idea grow roots:

> No one seems to have meditated seriously upon the fact that anywhere from one-third (recently) to one-half (historically) of all students admitted to Berkeley in any given year are held for Subject A, and that this situation has lasted for over 65 years. Most of these students are otherwise completely qualified to attend Berkeley. . . . To state that these students are ready for university work in all aspects but one is very puzzling indeed. Clearly something must be wrong with our definition of remedial work, or with our assessment of these students.[1]

I came across this observation a decade after Bartholomae uttered it, and a few years after I'd come to UC Berkeley and begun working with the students he mentions. I read his observation as an invitation to begin meditating seriously upon the phenomenon. In those meditations I was encouraged by UC Berkeley's Sarah Warshauer Freedman and Donald McQuade. Many thanks to both of them for their generosity in reading and commenting on drafts of the manuscript leading up to this book. Thanks also to Don McQuade for clarifying particular historical points, and for his good grace at those moments when my goals for the manuscript may have diverged from his hopes for it. Likewise, I am indebted to the anonymous reviewers of my manuscript whose incisive and productive suggestions were invaluable in my preparation of the final draft.

My primary "meditation hall" for this project was the Bancroft Library at UC Berkeley. I am indebted to the knowledgeable and unfailingly kind librarians of the Bancroft Archives for their professional guidance, and for their patience with my endless requests to paw through dusty documents. I am thankful for the good fortune of having worked with editor extraordinaire Dorine Jennette, whose intelligence, persistence, and good humor made the editing process a pleasure. I am grateful to my friends and colleagues at the College Writing Programs for many things, not the least of which was their encouragement of my work on this book. I am especially thankful to my colleague Caroline Cole. She read versions of several chapters and offered valuable perspective. She provided a valuable visual perspective, as well. Her gift, *The University of California, A Pictorial History*, one of her antiquarian bookstall finds, helped me see the faces behind the story, the posturing as well as the sheer presence of Berkeley's leaders, and the ramshackle buildings and tents on a weedy hill that that these leaders coaxed, dragged, inspired, and politicked into a great university.

Finally, everlasting thanks to Ann Stanley for every bit of all of it.

THE RHETORIC
OF REMEDIATION

INTRODUCTION

"To Embrace Every Child of California"

A toast to the University of California: To have laid its foundations broad enough to embrace every child of California that thirsts for knowledge!

Given at a banquet for legislators in February 1867, upon the occasion of their inspection visit to the proposed site for the university (Ferrier 1930, 284).

REMEDIAL WRITERS, like the poor, seem always to be with us.

It is more than passing strange, then, that programs and courses for these writers are almost always regarded as provisional by the institutions that offer them. With few exceptions, they are seen as special short-term measures to handle a crisis of illiteracy, or malliteracy, afflicting certain segments of the student body.

The crisis, in fact, has shown itself to have such remarkable staying power that the word *crisis* hardly applies. Throughout the 150-year history of composition instruction in American higher education, crises in students' literacy have been declared with regularity. The pronouncements have been so regular that composition scholars have been able to map these "crisis events" onto a larger American topography: crises in literacy correlate closely with moments of broad social change in American life, and with the concomitant expansion of college admission practices. A crisis

—or at least a rhetoric of crisis—develops when the academy moves to embrace a population of students who had not previously been seen as "college material."

The study of this rhetoric of crisis affords purchase on a delicate array of tensions that surround social class, race, entitlement, and access to higher education. Again and again, students' incapacity to deploy appropriate grammar or diction has been elided with their perceived inability to exercise taste, refinement, and even moral probity. For example, Harvard's Charles William Eliot expected, in 1869, that lessons designed to remedy students' errors in punctuation and paragraph structure would erect for them a "moral superstructure" (Douglas 1996, 129). Nearly a century later, the University of California's Clark Kerr, noting comparable sins of syntax, called for instruction in "the decencies."[1]

This peculiar elision of grammatical precision with moral fiber has been productively explored in composition scholarship. Richard Ohmann (1976) found it curious that students' writing became cause for alarm when the merchant class joined the social elite on campus, upsetting their long-held monopoly on higher education. James Berlin (1987) found similar dismay over grammatical infelicities when World War II veterans, many from the middle class, more than a few from the working class, crowded into college classrooms. Berlin also noted the emergence of a similar rhetoric of crisis when civil rights initiatives brought a new kind of student through the gates. David Russell (1992) observed the same species of rhetoric when young refugees from the Vietnam War reached college age.

As elsewhere, this correlation between the rhetoric of crisis and shifts in the student population is apparent in California. Complaints about college students' illiteracy are wholly correlatable with the population explosion on California's campuses created by the GI Bill in the immediate postwar years. Likewise, California's favored status as a destination for refugee and immigrant groups has given rise to the rhetoric of crisis around college students' literacy levels. Complaints about students' writing have served Californians just as well as they have served other Americans as a way to register publicly, if indirectly, dismay over the disruption of the social equilibrium caused by these new additions to the student body. For Californians, as for other Americans, the rhetoric of crisis was a way to confer dignity upon opinions about whom the gates to academia should bar.

Those gates get rattled mightily by the University of California's Mike Rose. In "The Language of Exclusion" (1985), he explores what he calls "the myth of transience" (341): the notion that, although a particularly unskilled and problematic group of students is pushing through the gates at a given moment, overturning the proprieties of prose, all will soon be well, and order will be restored to the academy. In Rose's view, this myth of transience is deeply entrenched in administrators' perceptions of student writers. This crisis thinking, Rose argues, is antithetical to the project of developing sustainably funded programs of instruction. The myth of transience fuels shortsighted planning, and localizes writing instruction to one or two composition courses. Worse, Rose believes, this myth effectively insulates the disciplines from the opportunity—and responsibility—to develop broad curricular responses to the needs of student writers. Finally, the myth of transience promotes what Sharon Crowley (1998) characterizes as a "composition-specialist underclass" (x), "temporary" faculty hired on a contingency basis year after year after year.

In her rich analysis of the history of remediation at City College of New York, Mary Soliday (2002), like Rose and others, challenges the notion that an institution's need to mount a remedial writing program is merely an ad hoc response to a temporary circumstance, to a demographic anomaly. Her case study forges compelling causal links between City College's literacy crises and the city's fiscal crises, and does much to explode the myth of transience. Drawing from Barbara Ann Scott's (1983) study of crisis management practices in universities, Soliday comes to see admissions policies and remediation programs as strategies to deal not only with demographic shifts, but also with the economic instability of boom-and-bust cycles.

Few states have ridden the boom-and-bust bronco as dramatically as has California, and her university began invoking the myth of transience as early as the 1880s, when instruction in composition (soon to be labeled "Subject A"[2]) was seen as a temporary solution to a shortcoming in precollegiate English instruction. The problem would dissolve, it was believed, just as soon as California's high school teachers heeded the copious advice that the University's English faculty pressed on them during their inspection visits to the schools.

This advice was later codified in the widely distributed publication *Suggestions to Teachers of English in the Secondary Schools* (1894), coauthored by Cornelius Beach Bradley, a former teacher at Oakland High School who joined the University of California's English faculty in 1883, and Charles Mills Gayley, an assistant professor of English at the University of Michigan who had been wooed away by California in 1887 (Kurtz 1943).

In "suggesting" curriculum and conducting inspection visits to California high schools in order to certify the quality of the coursework, these two men were following the practice established at Michigan during Gayley's tenure there. By 1870, the University of Michigan had organized its admission standards around a certification program predicated upon a book list specified by Michigan faculty. This certification program was established partly in response to complaints about the weak writing skills of Michigan's college entrants. Under this system, university faculty presented a list of texts and a curriculum to the high schools, and periodically sent professors to visit high school classrooms to certify that the curriculum was being followed.

Certification of high schools proved popular: the University of Minnesota established a certification system in 1871, Illinois and Indiana did so in 1872, and Ohio followed in 1874 (Rudolph 1962). Harvard issued its book list to secondary and prep schools in 1874, and the North East Commission of Colleges followed suit in 1884. Within three years, the Association of Colleges and Preparatory Schools of the Middle States and Maryland presented a certification plan based on a book list and visits from college faculty, and finally, in 1895, the National Conference on College Entrance Requirements was established to promulgate a booklist appropriate to all potential matriculants nationwide (Wechsler 1977). By 1900, nearly all state colleges and universities had a certification program, as did some 150 private colleges nationwide (Rudolph 1962).

Still, despite the popularity of these rigorously articulated programs of directing and inspecting high school curricula, college entrants continued to be a disappointment to their professors. The disappointment was most keenly felt—and loudly bemoaned—in the matter of students' writing. The tradition of certifying high schools continued, however, despite the evidence of its inefficacy, along with the tradition of complaint.

So too continued the tradition of seeing the "writing problem" as anomalous and temporary. As Mary Soliday crisply notes: "In the myth of transience, no group of students needs as much writing instruction as the group we currently serve" (2002, 11). Writing for *College English* back in

1938, Arthur Hudson identified this enduring and unquestioning perception as "the perennial problem of the ill-prepared" (728). Yet the University of California, like all its sisters in academe, continued to subscribe to the myth of transience throughout the early decades of the century and into the interwar years.

At California, the myth of transience was retold with particular vigor in the years following World War II, when the University's Committee on Educational Policy asserted that the problem with students' writing would abate with the departure of the large corps of war veterans who had enrolled with the aid of the GI Bill.[3] Later, in 1967, the myth of transience got a picturesque retelling when the chairman of the Committee on Subject A at the UC Berkeley campus voiced the sanguine expectation that the Subject A course would "expire from malnutrition."[4]

Notwithstanding that complacent prediction, instruction at UC Berkeley in basic composition (Subject A[5]) today is not even beginning to feel hunger pangs. The university's Subject A requirement is over one hundred years old, and remedial coursework has been heavily mandated for most of that century. For nearly every semester since 1869, some students have been found lacking in Subject A—that is, in composition skills—and have been "held" in one way or another for instruction. The proportion of students held for instruction has decreased substantially at the Berkeley campus over the last thirty years, though the decrease has been less dramatic in the rest of the University of California system. (In the 1970s UC Berkeley held roughly 50 percent of its students for Subject A; currently the figure averages about 20 percent. On the other hand, some 50 percent of students have been held, considering numbers across the entire University of California system, in recent years.)

According to the University of California's Glynda Hull, the Subject A requirement evidences a peculiar institutional ambivalence toward underprepared students. In "Alternatives to Remedial Writing: Lessons from Theory, from History, and a Case in Point," Hull (1999, 13) considers carefully the language of a report prepared in 1972 by the university's Committee on Educational Policy, hereafter called by its colloquial name, the Turner-Martin Report:

> One inevitable result of the University's generally admirable admission standards . . . is the admission each year of many students who are unable

to write a straightforward, literate answer to an essay examination in any college course.[6]

Here, and elsewhere in this report, Hull sees the university's ambivalent attitude toward underprepared students as "welcoming and marginalizing them in the same breath" (13). I'd like to propose that this ambivalence, like breathing, has been necessary (and autonomic) to the university. From its earliest days, the university has needed the construct of the remedial student to establish (and later, demonstrate) its status among other institutions of higher education. This is absolutely not to suggest that there is no such thing as an underprepared student or an improficient writer. The University of California (and every other institution) certainly enrolls some students each year whose academic future benefits greatly from the extra work in composition that they are asked to do. Few who work in composition would gainsay this.

Rather, I would suggest that the university's ability to label a group of students "remedial" is a powerful rhetorical tool. I hope to show in the following pages how this rhetorical tool has been wielded very successfully over the course of the university's history to define and defend its stature. I am convinced that the well-published lamentations about students' "illiteracy" (and later, "deficiency"; and later, "need for remediation"; and recently, "underpreparation") have accomplished important political—that is to say rhetorical—work for the university, and for California herself.

This claim is easiest to defend in a discussion of UC Berkeley's—and California's—early history, when the wild young state struggled for legitimacy among her more stable elders. I begin by telling the story of the curious administrative accommodation that allowed the cash-strapped young University of California to accept nearly all applicants, but at the same time to identify half of them as illiterate.

The University of California was not alone, in the nineteenth and early twentieth century, in accepting nearly everyone who had the means to buy a place at the university. Educational historian Harold Wechsler (1977) characterizes it as "inconceivable" in those times that any college or university had the "luxury" of choosing only the most qualified applicants (8). The University of California *was* alone, however, in the remarkable—

and very public—way its head of English, Charles Mills Gayley, made lemonade of these lemons.

Gayley (1895) asserted rather peculiar bragging rights over these students who were accepted despite their apparent unacceptability. In 1894, the widely read literary and cultural magazine the *Dial* published "English in American Universities, by Professors in the English Departments of Twenty Representative Institutions." In his contribution to the series, describing the University of California's curricular demands, Gayley insisted that, although the secondary school preparation of California's young aspirants to higher education was far more thoroughgoing than that offered to young people in many eastern states, their training still was not as thorough as would be necessary for them to benefit fully from all the university had to offer. In his paean to the University of California's high standards—higher, apparently, than the eastern states'—Gayley did not remind readers that these high standards were unconnected to acceptance. He neglected to mention that applicants whose accomplishments fell short of the university's aspirations were enrolled—enveloped, as it were—in a disdainful embrace.

California's aspirants to higher education were not the first young people to find themselves embraced and disgraced. As early as 1871, the brilliant and politically astute James Angell used the occasion of his inauguration as president of the University of Michigan to complain that entrants' disappointing proficiency levels prevented faculty from "do[ing] work of real university grade" (Kitzhaber 1990, 29). And Harvard, just three years before Gayley's adulatory yet condemnatory claim about California's college-bound youth, characterized the task of working with students' writing as "stupefying" and an "obviously absurd" misuse of Harvard's faculty and funds.[7]

Next, my story rewinds several decades to consider the rhetorical ground from which Professor Gayley's audacious claim of 1895 bloomed. I assay the bleak economic conditions that gripped California during the closing quarter of the nineteenth century, and the equally bleak prospects for her university's success: both agriculture and education battled drought conditions in California during those years.

Writing in 1883, four years before Gayley arrived from Michigan, and twelve years before that claim in the *Dial*'s "English in American Universities" series about California's students, Professor Cornelius Beach Bradley mourned the grave ineptitude of generations of composition students, constructing a student population as "unfortunate, lazy, and feeble-minded."[8] Bradley's lament, though particularly pungent, was not novel. Rather, it was the latest entry in a national competition of complaint begun back in 1837, when students of America's first public university, North Carolina, were declared wanting in their ability to write clearly and intelligently (Hudson 1938). In 1879, no less a luminary than Adams Sherman Hill, Boylston Professor of Rhetoric and founder, in 1872, of Harvard's composition program, summed up the complaints of his forebears in an address to secondary school teachers: "Every one who has had much to do with the graduating classes of our best colleges has known men who could not write a letter describing their own Commencement without making blunders which would disgrace a boy twelve years old" (Brereton 1995, 46).

Everyone who had much to do with the *entering* classes knew young men (and women) whose blunders would disgrace their high school English teachers. Since colleges and universities, particularly public ones, could ill afford to disappoint these disappointing applicants, an accommodation called "conditioning" was created. Conditioning served not only pedagogical aims, but also political and pecuniary ones. Under this accommodation, students who had passed their entrance exams in some subjects but failed in others were offered conditional acceptance, and given a grace period (typically a year) in which to acquire proficiency in the subjects they had failed.

Swiftly, a great number of students were cast into that dubious state of grace. Like certification, the practice of conditioning readily gained currency nationwide. Historian Harold Wechsler (1977) estimates that by 1905, conditioning was widely practiced in both public and private institutions. So widespread was the practice of conditioning that the Carnegie Foundation for the Advancement of Teaching was moved that year to characterize the practice as "indiscriminate charity" (Wechsler 1977, 73).

The University of California was well ahead of the curve in the practice of this "charity," whereby students were declared unworthy of acceptance yet accepted anyway. In its first year, 1869, when the university was little more than a few rooms on a muddy hill with a student body of thirty-nine, a conditioned caste was created.

In 1883, when California's Professor of Rhetoric Cornelius Beach Bradley was charging his students with feeblemindedness, and levying conditions upon them, the legislature was attacking the university and threatening to withhold funds. California's legislators charged that the university was actually doing a disservice to the state by offering a curriculum *too elevated* for most of California's higher-education seekers. This charge by California's legislators would not have been unfamiliar to legislators of many states who grappled with the political unpalatability of levying taxes to support higher education. What would have been unfamiliar, however, was the remarkable way University of California President Horace Davis responded to it.

President Davis resolved this disjuncture of educational standards brilliantly. He performed nothing less than a feat of academic-political alchemy on this intellectual dross that Professor Bradley had so deplored, turning it into pure gold for the university. President Davis argued that the very existence of so many unsatisfactory students was prima facie evidence that the university desperately needed the legislature's strong support if California were to drag upward the intellectual level of its youth. This argument was, of course, an early instantiation of the rhetoric of remediation. In California in 1883, then, it might be more accurate to say that the practice of conditioning was not so much indiscriminate charity as strategic charity.

But that was then.

It would be easy to read these remarkable feats of statebuilding sleight of hand as no more than an artifact of California's and her university's early days. A one-off. An example of the brilliance and opportunism that built California. Yet I will pick up the trail of this rhetoric of remediation in the early decades of the twentieth century. Between 1890 and 1900, enrollments at state universities throughout the nation nearly doubled, and they had nearly doubled again by 1920 (Brereton 1995). California's economy in particular had begun to thrive and California's taxpayers were clamoring for higher education for their offspring.

The university had more than enough students to justify its existence to the legislature. In fact, in the late 1890s, University of California President Wheeler characterized the press of students clamoring for places at his university as "an avalanche" (Douglass 2000, 107). It wasn't only

Wheeler's university, though. It was California's, and demands for access from her young people, seconded by their taxpaying parents, had to be accommodated. Also demanding accommodation was President Wheeler's fierce ambition—fueled by competition from an energetic and rich young Stanford just down the road—that the callow young state campus at the foot of the hill in Berkeley become nothing less than a "world university" (Ferrier 1930, 444). Wheeler's struggle to accommodate California's students along with his own ambitions posed a by-now familiar dilemma: how could the university accept more students than ever, all the while insisting that its academic standards were higher than ever?

Wheeler's solution was to float a rather disingenuous interpretation of the university's requirements. This interpretation resulted in the admission of an unprecedented number of students, and Wheeler's accommodation of that "avalanche" endeared him to Progressive, education-minded Governor Hiram Johnson. With Governor Johnson's support, Wheeler's university began its march toward "world university" status. Of the freshmen whom Wheeler welcomed, fully half were deemed illiterate, and were remanded to the custody of the so-called Committee on the Treatment of Incompetent Students. Once again, less-prepared (a.k.a. "incompetent") students were embraced and yet disdained, enabling the university to assert its high standards, yet, at the same time, to accept all the students it needed to in order to meet its political responsibilities.

In the 1930s, the dilemma was the same, but by then the university's administration had changed, as had the nature of its competition for the state's higher education dollars. Robert Gordon Sproul presided over the University of California during the Great Depression, and, like every other president of a public university or college, he had to contend with sharply diminished allocations for higher education. President Sproul bore an even heavier burden throughout the Depression and beyond: he struggled to suppress fervid legislative interest in developing a rival system of regional colleges. Such a system of regional colleges, the legislators hoped, would provide a more practical, populist education, a much-needed antidote to · the elitist university in those desperate times.

Sproul insisted that there be but one university, and he fought tirelessly against what he called "little replicas" (Stadtman 1970, 158). He had the delicate rhetorical task of persuading the public that the university was "a genuinely democratic institution," while insisting that it must strive to strengthen its standards, as a service to California and "to the careers and happiness . . . of its young men and women" (Douglass 2000, 145). In short, Sproul's university had to be both democratic and elitist. If it failed "to embrace every child of California that thirsts for knowledge," it risked fueling the fever for regional colleges.

In an effort to limit the scope of that embrace, while still demonstrating the university's populism, President Sproul made common cause with the high schools. Once again, the construct of the remedial student proved invaluable in helping the University of California negotiate the line between accessibility and elitism. The university's Committee on Subject A was urged to rethink whether the composition exam was properly objective in its assessment of what students had learned in high school. The committee decided to add a section with questions on grammar and usage. The new exam was first administered in 1930, and it resulted in the highest pass rate in the university's history. Fewer students were suspected of illiteracy that year and remanded for treatment. However, the redefinition of the remedial student didn't help President Sproul remediate his university as a more populist institution. The accusations of elitism stuck; the legislature stood firm in its determination to establish regional colleges.

The University of California experienced enormous growth during and immediately after World War II. Every American institution of postsecondary learning felt this enrollment pressure, but the land grant universities and colleges in each state were particularly pressed to expand their enrollments. The University of California's members felt a different kind of expansion, as well—an expanding awareness of the University of California's importance as a resource to the nation, as an engine of research.

War veterans, bankrolled by the GI Bill, applied in record numbers to California's colleges and universities. By that time, President Sproul had lost his war on the regional colleges, the "little replicas" he so deplored. California's many regional colleges had grown into state colleges or universities, and were well placed to accept the veterans, as well as the federal funding that accompanied them. The University of California struggled to accommodate as many veterans as it could, even deciding to relax its admission standards temporarily. This decision was borne of patriotism, surely, but also of prudence, given the fact that the gates to these new state colleges and universities—those little replicas—swung open wider and with far less noise than did the gates of the University of California.

In the aftermath of the war, however, the University of California was still dodging bullets. President Sproul feared the diversion of the university's resources to the "little replicas," and he worried about the dilution of the university's status as it competed with those replicas for money and students. Sproul had a potent weapon in this war; he worked hard to assert the university's standards against those of the state's four-year public colleges. As before, new students' dismal writing proficiency was offered up as evidence of the university's high standards. The invading horde was welcomed, but complained about vigorously and publicly.

The postwar years saw another assault on the University of California's reputation. The loyalty oath controversy of 1949 through 1951 brought low the university and its president. In those early years of the "Communist menace," President Sproul tried to quash the University of California's (especially the Berkeley campus's) reputation as the "Red University," and the resulting furor dimmed the luster that the war years had conferred upon it.

Clark Kerr's appointment as the Berkeley campus's first chancellor in the wake of the loyalty oath debacle brought his efforts to restore UC Berkeley's reputation among universities—and among taxpayers. In those years, the legislature was asking prickly questions about why it should fund higher education's freshman and sophomore years three times: at the state's junior colleges, at her four-year colleges, and at the University of California. An even pricklier question was put to the University of California by the legislature: why were its "13th and 14th grades" so much costlier than those offered by the other institutions?

This was a tight spot for the university to be in. It swiftly strove to impress the legislature and the public with the idea that those thirteenth and fourteenth years of instruction on offer at the junior colleges and four-year colleges were inferior to those available at the university. The university chose this moment to take note of the copious complaints among its faculty about the low proficiency levels of transfer students who had done their thirteenth and fourteenth years in the junior colleges. The university was particularly attentive to complaints that transfer students had not learned to write properly. A "Prose Improvement Project" was established at UC Berkeley, and a number of committees were appointed to take up the "Subject A problem."

The Prose Improvement Project might well have exceeded its portfolio, however. It quickly moved beyond consideration of transfer students' problems and the implicit deficiencies of instruction in the thirteenth and fourteenth grades at the other state schools. Rather, the Prose Improvement Project asserted that students do not learn writing once and for all in freshman year. Writing instruction, they insisted, must be the focus of all academic departments across all four years. This is an important observation in the history of composition, of course, and it anticipated by twenty-some years the development of the writing-across-the-disciplines movement. It was not, however, an assertion that helped the University of California promote that complicated dual agenda of accessibility and elitism: its accessibility to transfer students, and its elite status as having expectations that exceeded those students' attainments.

In 1951 the Liaison Committee on the Subject A Problem was formed to consider the shortcomings in transfer students' writing. The committee made two recommendations, both of which were politically fraught. First, they recommended that the Subject A exam be used in deciding admissions, rather than as a tool for placing already-admitted students into the appropriate composition course. Subject A had been a placement tool for most of the university's life, and the Academic Senate of 1951 quickly found a compelling reason why it should remain so. They discovered that males had a higher likelihood of failing the exam, and that, if it were to become an entrance requirement, the University of California would have to admit substantially more females than males. This outcome, they declared, was "to be looked at askance."[9] The recommendation was promptly withdrawn. The second recommendation of the Special Committee on the Subject A Problem was that transfer students be required to take the Subject A exam even if they had completed the composition requirement at a junior college before entering the university. This proposal was understood, reasonably enough, as an affront to the politically emergent junior college system. It too was withdrawn.

The passage into law of the Master Plan for Higher Education brought with it the triumphal rehabilitation of the University of California. The Master Plan was in large part the brainchild of Clark Kerr, who by that time had moved from chancellor of the Berkeley campus to president of the University of California system. The university's and California's celebration was cut short, however, as the FBI began its coruscating investigation into the lives and professional practices of the university's—especially UC Berkeley's and UCLA's—administrators, faculty members, and students. FBI Director Hoover was at the height of his powers and full exercise of his whims in those years, and, bizarrely, the Subject A exam was among the unsavory aspects of the University of California that drew his fire. As I will detail, one of the exam questions roused his ire, and Subject A committee members found themselves on an FBI suspects list.

UC Berkeley students made the list as well, having demonstrated in San Francisco at hearings of the House Un-American Activities Committee in 1959. This student activism was followed by demonstrations that grew into the watershed free speech movement. Gubernatorial candidate Ronald Reagan fumed through the free speech movement, and then Governor Reagan positively exploded when UC Berkeley students demonstrated to preserve People's Park. Reagan vowed "to rid the campus of disruptive elements, at the point of a bayonet, if necessary" (Rorabaugh 1989, 66). Prime among those disruptive elements, in Governor Reagan's view, was the university's president, Clark Kerr.

In the intense drama of the free speech movement, of course, Subject A performed no more than a walk-on role in the first act. Governor Reagan performed the leading role, and by the time the curtain rang down, Berkeley's and Clark Kerr's golden ages were over. Soon enough, the Vietnam War and attendant student activism were in full swing, and a new wave of public complaint was focused on the moral and intellectual laxity of students. One of the myriad manifestations of this complaint was increased scrutiny of Subject A and the remedial student.

Thus arrived a new era of widespread complaint about students' writing abilities. California was only one locus of a national upheaval about standards, remediation, and access to higher education. California was, in fact, a continent away from the epicenter of that upheaval, the City College of New York. City College's historic—and historically repercussive—response to the call for expanded access to higher education ignited a firestorm of rhetoric about remediation that began in New York, but ultimately consumed the attention of politicians, public intellectuals, pundits, college presidents, educators, and compositionists across the nation.[10] In California, firestorms are known to seed the growth of new forests, but this western phenomenon was observed in New York City when the basic writing movement was born from the flames. California felt the heat in a very public way in 1975 when a *Newsweek* feature entitled "Why Johnny Can't Write" (Sheils 1975) memorialized the low attainments of student writers at UC Berkeley, and fatefully attached the name "Bonehead English" to UC Berkeley's remedial writing course.

Cultural tensions surrounding gender and race entered the equation during this time, as renewed interest arose at UC Berkeley in making Subject A an entrance exam. Once again, the specter of admitting more women than men was raised; once again, the proposal died. Moreover, charges of racism were levied in the 1970s against the Subject A Office and its affiliate, the Subject A Office for Non-native Speakers of English (SANSE). The Subject A and SANSE faculty members successfully and unequivocally defended themselves against the accusation that their instruction and attitudes forced Asian American students "to compromise their cultural loyalties," and other charges.[11] The Academic Senate lauded the Subject A and SANSE programs for their work. Notwithstanding that praise, the Asian American Studies Program was granted authority to teach a special Subject A course judged appropriate for Asian American students.

Thus began an odd transfer of the embrace-and-disgrace phenomenon that has been described in earlier chapters. Via these Academic Senate hearings, the Subject A *faculty* members were placed into that uncomfortable category that heretofore had been occupied by their *students*. The faculty members were adjudged a necessary and important presence in a democratic university, and their work was praised. Yet their ability to offer appropriate and sensitive instruction to Asian American students was found wanting. To steal the words offered by Professor Gayley (1895) over a century ago about the remedial student, the Subject A faculty's work, though nothing less than heroic, "was just not up to the mark" (Brereton 1995, 169).

The 1980s saw an increase in the number of University of California students for whom English was a second (or third) language, and throughout the 1970s and 1980s, California's poor economic health impacted the University. These two demographic developments produced a compound result. Proportionately speaking, more low-income, minority, and immigrant students than ever before were being admitted, and, in general, they had encountered less preparation for college-level work, and had less fluency in English, than their predecessors.[12] Not surprisingly, this situation exacerbated the complaints from faculty that they "were being asked to handle problems, especially in writing, that they were never trained to handle."[13]

University of California President David Saxon, like his predecessors, was bound by the ethos of mass access to higher education, the duty to provide instruction appropriate for *all* the students the university accepts, and by the conflicting need to maintain the high standards expected of this proud university. Confronted with the threat of severe budget cuts, and mindful of the chorus of complaints, President Saxon commissioned a study of the cost of Subject A instruction, its extent, and the possibility of outsourcing it to the university's extension program or to the community colleges.

The findings convinced Saxon that Subject A was an essential component of on-campus instruction, given California's demographics. Saxon also remained convinced that Subject A coursework was plainly remedial, even though, at that time, over 55 percent of the students who had qualified fully for admission were identified as requiring Subject A instruction. University of California Senate Resolution 633(D), enacted during President Saxon's administration, made clear the disdain in that embrace: students who placed into Subject A courses were to be considered remedial, no matter what percentage of the freshman class they constituted, and they would face dismissal if they did not solve their writing problems by the end of the freshman year.

The external review of the Subject A program that was undertaken at UC Berkeley in 1989 had far-reaching results, particularly in response to another charge of racism and discriminatory behavior and policy toward Asian-ancestry students. As before, the members of the external review committee found no evidence of intentional racism or discriminatory behavior. Additionally, they made a brace of recommendations intended to demolish the program's identity as remedial, to refresh what they labeled a "stale curriculum," to raise faculty morale, and to bring Subject A instruction and faculty into closer communication with departments offering composition courses.[14] Their recommendations included the establishment of the College Writing Programs, to be directed by a ladder-rank faculty member with research interests in composition, and offering credit-bearing courses.

In 1991, University of California President David Gardner mandated that all remedial instruction be removed from the university's campuses. UC Berkeley's institutional response was to implement the recommendations of the external review committee. The College Writing Programs were brought into being through the strenuous efforts of then-Dean Donald McQuade, professor of English and veteran composition specialist; Glynda Hull, professor of education and composition specialist; and Arthur Quinn, professor of rhetoric and founding director of the College Writing Programs. The programs' first curricular move was to combine Subject A-level instruction with instruction in first-year freshman composition into a single, intensive, accelerated, six-unit course that the university credited as "non-remedial." This protected Subject A instruction from removal from campus in response to President Gardner's mandate. Thus was the ghost of remediation exorcised.

Quinn became the first ladder-rank faculty director in 1992, and he shepherded the faculty through the transition from Subject A to College Writing Programs. He oversaw the complex curricular and cultural shifts entailed in that transformation. Hull became the College Writing Programs' director in 1995, and began initiatives to further increase the faculty's and the programs' participation in writing instruction beyond Subject A. These initiatives included the development of advanced composition courses, and the appointment of some new faculty with PhDs in composition/rhetoric. It is during this period in the history of Subject A that the ghost of remediation seemed finally to have been laid to rest.

However, the circumstances of the mid-1990s—economic and demographic—resurrected that ghost, or rather, the haunting was relocated. This time, the complaints about students' improficient writing were lodged against juniors and seniors, rather than incoming freshmen. This concluding part of the history is testament to the persistent—and resistant—power of the rhetoric of remediation, and a final meditation on the purpose this rhetoric serves.

A close examination of the history of composition instruction and of the institutional discourse surrounding it demonstrates that the rhetoric of remediation has persisted throughout the century, encoded at the University of California in the Subject A apparatus. As I worked my way through the University of California archives and the Subject A archives, I came to see the discourse of remediation as incantatory language that wafts through a century of discussions at UC Berkeley. It revealed itself to me repeatedly in the records of the university that I consulted—the memoirs, the memories, the minutes, the minutiae.

The documents that I examined included the minutes of the academic council and senate; records of committees on courses, on educational policy, on student prose, on student preparation, on remedial matters, on affirmative action; reports of task forces; findings of blue-ribbon panels; letters of complaint penned by University of California presidents, chancellors, professors, taxpayers; and accounts in the popular press, and in memoirs of university luminaries. The earliest documents that I examined were written in 1867, the most recent in 2006. I strove to examine all relevant materials between those years.

The discursive network of these records is dense; it yielded some quite remarkable blasts from the past—and bleats—that taught me to prick up my ears to the connection between matters of proficiency and matters of purse strings, between concern for standards and concern for stature. In *Politics of Remediation* (2002), Soliday exhorts us to look harder into institutional and ideological arrangements to understand why for "over a century faculty and administrators in every segment of private and public higher education have skirmished over writing curriculums, complained about student writing, and lamented the decline of standards" (3). The chapters that follow attempt to shine a light on (and, I hope, through) the University of California, Berkeley's particular skirmishes, complaints, and lamentations around student writing. This book will, I hope, document that university's place as a stage upon which the rhetoric of remediation was enacted with particular art. And artifice.

This story of the rhetoric of remediation at UC Berkeley will, I hope, be read as an illustrative case study of the dynamics of remediation; the fluid, complex nature of standards; and the myriad ways in which the decisions about students' attainments as writers can be seen as responses to prevailing political, economic, and social forces.

In *The Politics of Writing Instruction: Postsecondary* (1991), John Trimbur posits the following: "To think of literacy crises as ideological events is to think rhetorically . . ." (281). I hope that my effort to describe this perduring rhetorical phenomenon at Berkeley will encourage fellow compositionists to consider their institution's own rhetoric of remediation, with particular attention to the complex purposes it may have served, and may continue to serve.

CHAPTER 1

"The Honor of
the State"

> The most broadly and thoroughly planned
> scheme [of instruction in English], that is
> in force at the University of California, is, in
> many respects different from the common
> Eastern type, and deserves the careful study
> of teachers throughout the country.
>
> *Professor G. R. Carpenter (1895) of Columbia
> College, commenting in the* Educational
> Review *on Charles Mills Gayley's (1895) article
> in the* Dial.

IN ITS EARLY YEARS, the Subject A requirement enabled the University of
California to separate the sheep from the goats, English-wise, but the separation had more symbolic than practical use. The university was committed to granting admission to both the 50 percent who passed the exam in
composition, and to their less proficient brethren,[1] the 50 percent who
failed. There were strong political reasons for this: the University of California was a public institution, after all, endowed through the Morrill Act to
serve the education needs of future engineers, agriculturists, and mechanics
—a group of applicants arguably underrepresented among the top 50 percent in composition proficiency. The state's university had been crafted
from the rib of the College of California, established in 1864 as a private
institution following a largely classical curriculum. When the College of
California became California's public university in 1869, it continued, at
first, in the curricular footsteps of the institution that had given it life.

Very quickly, however, taxpayer pressures were brought to bear. The Grangers represented one threat to the university's access to Morrill Act funds and to state monies; a political force of some consequence, they objected to Berkeley's largely classical curriculum, complaining that the students who came to study agriculture were lured away by Latin, Greek, and the siren call of modern languages (Ferrier 1930).

The administration of this young institution could hardly turn its back on these petitioners for admission. But it could look down its nose. It could signal its disappointment with them, thereby affirming the university's high standards. This practice, which Hull calls "welcoming and marginalizing," is well-nigh irresistible from the point of view of a struggling young university. Such a rhetorical posture demonstrates that the university is serving California's citizens, even welcoming some of her questionable students, but at the same time upholding its standards, asserting its status, by marginalizing these students.

From its very first semester in 1869, the University of California enrolled two categories of students. One category was simply top drawer; these were the students whose passage through the university was unquestioned—pending, of course, the sedulous application of effort. Yet the other category of students could not be called "bottom drawer": in the early years of the university, the sole purpose of California's secondary schools, tellingly called "feeder schools" by University of California faculty, was to prepare students for the university. The true bottom drawer, those students who didn't get into the University of California after having prepped in Latin, Greek, and ancient history at secondary schools, were not particularly disadvantaged; they frequently went directly into San Francisco to help tend to their fathers' businesses, or to the Sierras to help tend to their fathers' mines. (Much later the University of California was reconstructed, one might say "Kerred,"[2] so as to prevent any possibility of contact with the bottom drawer, and legislated, famously, to draw its student population from the upper 12.5 percent of California's secondary school graduates.) This second-class category, then, students whose presence at the university raised eyebrows, but was tolerated, we might provisionally call the "middle drawer."

In the early years, the university had a benign enough label for these second-class people: "conditioned students." Conditioning was widely practiced in both public and private universities during the second half of the nineteenth century and into the early twentieth. The practice was especially prevalent on the public campuses of the Midwest and West Coast, where budget shortfalls and taxpayer demands compelled registrars to serve as "unquestioning hosts" (Taylor 1928). At the University of California, students could be conditioned in subjects other than composition; for example, in its inaugural year, of the thirty-eight students accepted, more than a few were conditioned in various subjects, including geography and history.[3] By this administrative sorting system, the university's agreement to render these people full citizens of the academic community was conditioned upon their proving their worthiness in those subjects.

The institutional language around this admissions practice suggested that conditions had solidity, heft: students were said to "lift" the condition by successfully completing an exam, or were described as "carrying" conditions. The record is not clear as to the number of conditioned students who were dismissed from the university for having lifted inadequately. There were two ways to be dismissed from the University of California in those years, so soon after the Civil War: a person could be honorably discharged or dishonorably discharged.[4] The record does not indicate into which group was cast the conditioned student who failed to lift his burden.

It should be noted that applicants who proposed to carry a *very* heavy load of conditions into the university were denied entrance, but the load had to be especially onerous, as the University of California, like other universities and colleges, was struggling to build enrollment during the serious economic and social crises of the 1870s, and couldn't afford to be too choosy. UC's conditioned students, the middle drawer, were valuable resources. Their fees helped defray operating expenses during the 1880s, when the legislature was uninterested in underwriting secondary schools, let alone a state university. And, of course, they provided evidence that the new university had standards. In a young state (recall that gold was discovered at Sutter's Mill a mere twenty years before the University of California opened its doors), with an unusually egalitarian sensibility and not a great popular affection for the life of the mind, the university had some heavy lifting of its own to do, just to prove its worth. We might say that the citizens of this new, "golden" state had accepted the university, but with conditions.

By the 1890s the label "conditioned student" had disappeared at UC and the enrollment crisis had passed. Taking its lead from the University of Michigan, UC had developed an elaborate system wherein professors visited secondary school classrooms, quizzing students and teachers, and awarding accreditation to those subjects that had passed their scrutiny. Often, but not always, secondary schools were given full accreditation in all subjects; in some cases, accreditation would be denied for particular subjects. In cases like these, applicants to the university had to sit for exams in the subjects for which their secondary school had not received accreditation. Excepting these occasional special cases, by the turn of the century, the only subject that remained a complete disappointment to the professoriat of the university was English. The university's Committee on Relations with Schools was in a near-continuous state of public dismay over the shortcomings that they perceived in applicants' writing.

The institutional solution to this difficulty was that the middle drawer was now defined as the 50 percent of students who failed the examination in English, quibbles with high schools over geography or algebra instruction having been resolved by accreditation, or by the university's reduction of its entrance requirements, which formerly had mirrored Harvard's. Thus was the middle drawer repacked. It became a commonplace that California's secondary schools (by now totaling ninety-eight) were successfully instructing her most promising young citizens in all subjects *except* English composition. This claim put California comfortably in context with its more advanced sister states. The University of California could join with the University of Michigan or the University of Chicago in their complaints about the widespread and shocking deficiency of so many young people in their writing abilities. California's young people were just as good—or bad—as Michigan's or Illinois'. As were, by extension, her high schools and her university. The middle drawer brought California parity with her older sisters.

In UC's early years, then, the student held for Subject A did far more than refine his grammar. I would suggest that this "deficient" 50 percent of the student body shouldered a not-inconsiderable share of the burden of building the university. That is, the rhetoric that compelled him to "lift" his conditions in Subject A also lifted the status of the university in the eyes of California's citizens and others. In turn, the university was asked to play a leading role in building the state, making it a place where people would want to settle and raise their families. Without that deficient 50 percent who were constructed from the rhetoric of remediation, the pitiful assembly of a few buildings on the muddy hill above Bancroft Avenue in Berkeley might never have attained the critical mass it needed to become a viable institution. As the press saw it, in the matter of nourishing a university, "the honor of the state is involved" (Ferrier 1930, 378).

California may have had abundant gold in those early years, but it was far from a "Golden State" when the university was established. California society of the time has been described as possessed of "a restless character, speculative temper," and a passion for "the relentless pursuit of self interest" (Barth 1994, 2). The rampant street violence in San Francisco in the early 1870s gave the language a new word, *hoodlum*.[5] Californian existence was seen as one of "desperation, defeat, and lonely dying" (Starr 1981, 82). J. W. Boddam-Whetham, an English naval officer in port in San Francisco in 1870, writes in his diary of seeing a man who had lost his fortune in a mining debacle shoot his brains out in the street (Boddam-Whetham 1874, 174–75).

In 1876, seven years into the university's life, California is described as "full of social wrecks—wrecks more complete than any possible in calmer seas. There is said to be a greater proportion of suicides here than anywhere else in the civilized world" (Fisher 1876, 72–73). In *Afoot and Alone*, Stephen Powers laments that "this darling and sunny child of our young Republic is already as old as Europe in suicide" (Powers 1872, 324). Even the *Annals of San Francisco*, though commissioned to attract settlers, cannot help but sketch California as a belligerent, unpredictable youth, rather than a sunny child. California, admits the *Annals*, is known in the East to infect its arrivals with a "restless, morbid desire for change, excitement, and wild adventure" (Soulé 1849, 289). Hardly the place to attract families, settlers, the yeoman farmer so cherished by the founders of the young Republic.

The Resources of California, published in 1863, regards California's proclivity to attract schemers rather than settlers as fatal to its development: "Most men in California do not live here to enjoy life, but to make money so that they may enjoy life in some other country" (Hittell 1863, 452–53). Horace Bushnell, a New England cleric intent on making California the

Massachusetts of the Coast, both in piety and in education, saw the university as a central force in dispelling that social anomie. In "Appeal to the Public," a speech delivered to the trustees of the College of California on January 20, 1857, Bushnell predicted, "Until they came together in the creation of a university, Californians would never become a people in the proper and organic sense of that term" (Ferrier 1930, 174).

The journalistic record of the times underscores the university's role in building the state. The *Occidental* editorialized that the university would "make the Coast attractive to all who may think of it as home" (January 18, 1868). The *San Francisco Evening Bulletin's* expectations for the university were more specific: "What Michigan University is now doing for the West, we hope to see the University of California do for the Coast" (March 17, 1869).

By the end of the nineteenth century, the University of California had done quite a lot for the coast, arguably more than the University of Michigan had done for the "West," since California's reputation as a worthy place to live needed so much more remediation than did Michigan's.

Fervidly active in remediating California's reputation as a clean, well-lighted place for books, and in remediating UC's student writers, was Charles Mills Gayley, who was recruited from Michigan to join the English faculty in 1889. Gayley was perhaps Berkeley's earliest charismatic professor. His Great Books lectures were so popular that larger venues had constantly to be found to accommodate the growing number of students enrolled (Stewart 1968).

A man of parts, Gayley was the author of numerous football cheer songs ("Zip la la / Boom rah rah / Class of 1900!") and a close friend of William James, whom he persuaded to visit Berkeley. James is said to have presented for the first time the fundamentals of his philosophy of pragmatism at a public lecture here (Kurtz 1943). Gayley's 1894 report on the University of California, first written for the *Dial* and included in William Payne's influential series *English in American Universities* (Gayley 1895), is itself a classic study in the rhetoric of remediation, the contemptuous embrace so crucial to this young university's stature, and thus, the state's.

In his report, Gayley (1895) boasts that California is unique among the states in requiring the applicants to her university to prepare themselves to be examined not only in Latin and Greek, but in Norse mythology and the Teutonic sagas. Gayley insisted that the requirements of the New England Association of Colleges "are similar to those of California, but they do not go more than two-thirds of the way in extent or in stringency" (168). Beyond the Norse myths, Gayley claimed, applicants worthy of admission to the University of California were expected to have prepped themselves in at least three of Burke's orations, and the course in argument, as well as "some twenty-five of the longer masterpieces" of English poetry (169).

Sadly, (and oddly, Gayley's tone suggests) the work done by California's young people, though nothing less than heroic, was just "not up to the mark." It was up to the university to impose in the secondary schools and in the university itself "supervision so minute" (169) that California would soon be worthy to step up to her heritage as the Massachusetts of the Pacific. This minute supervision would exact its toll on the university's faculty, Gayley intimated, referring to the "disgust" occasioned by reading students' compositions (169), but this price was not too great if it redounded to the greater glory of California.

Gayley's report worked its rhetorical magic, laying California's claim to greatness by lamenting the failings of her students, the same students whose meticulous academic preparation he had just lauded. It is a curious sleight of hand that Gayley engaged in for the *Dial*, rather like a father complaining to the relatives that though his son was a star athlete, the lad still had to be scolded for neglecting to dust the trophies.

Indeed there is some suggestion in the official records of the University of California's admissions requirements during Gayley's time that he may have engaged in a bit of California mythologizing; California's youth seem not to have been prepped quite as rigorously as he indicated, and her university's demands not as stringent. But the facts are less important than the effect of his claim. Gayley might have gilded the university's reputation a bit in overstating her standards and exaggerating the faculty's disgust at its less-prepared student writers, but California decidedly gained luster from his claim in the nationally circulated periodical, the *Dial*.

CHAPTER 2

"The Unfortunate, the Lazy, and the Feeble-Minded"

> We Californians make but poor figures
> in our daily walk and conversations.
> Foundations for higher growth we sadly
> lack. Ideals we have none. Philistines we
> are in soul most thoroughly.
>
> *Josiah Royce, English Department, in a letter
> to his patron, G. B. Coale, 1878. UC Berkeley
> Library Archives (Starr 1981, 151).*

THE UNIVERSITY OF CALIFORNIA may have been ushered grandiloquently onto the national stage by Charles Mills Gayley's rhetorical tour de force in the *Dial* in 1895, but the work done behind the proscenium, in the classroom and examination hall in the two decades before Gayley's arrival on the scene tells a compelling backstory.

In 1883, Cornelius Beach Bradley took up a place in the classroom, and most particularly the examination hall, at UC. It was a small English faculty that Bradley joined that year, as both Edward Rowland Sill and Josiah Royce had just shaken the dust of California off their spats and returned to the East. Sill had been head of UC's English Department nearly from the beginning. He had arrived in 1860 fresh from Yale, but with misgivings, warning a friend "I could not live long here—no culture, no thought, no art" (Starr 1981, 152). Sill surprised himself and his eastern friends by managing to stay on for twenty-some years. Nevertheless, he counted his time at UC a defeat. Of his work with students at Berkeley, he wrote, "I lost the battle for poetry and the battle for culture" (Starr, 152). In the end, he saw California and her university as plunged into a "Cimmerian Darkness" (Starr 1981, 152).

He had a point. California, by the end of the century, was reaping the rancid harvest of a generation raised in a squalid system of tenant farming (Starr 1981). Far from the "educated yeomanry of the land" sought by UC Professor of Agriculture Edward James Wickson, California agriculture was largely a plantation economy, with 63 percent of the land held by 7 percent of the population (Starr 1985). Journalist Henry George's indictment in *Our Land and Land Policy, National and State* (1871) is stark:

> California began under a cloud of greed, of perjury, of corruption, of spoliation, and high-handed robbery for which it will be difficult to find a parallel . . . Instead of sturdy farmers and mechanics, depression and land-lessness has reduced California's population to a debased condition more shiftless, perhaps than that of any state. (1)

This ruinous pattern of vast landholdings can be considered a consequence of the U.S. government's systematic contempt for the terms of the Treaty of Guadalupe Hidalgo. Under that agreement, Mexican small-holders in California—*Californios*—were to retain title to their *rancherias*. However, U.S. Senator William Gwyn, a California Republican, managed to shepherd legislation through Congress that effectively clouded these titles. This forced displaced *Californios* into generations of litigation that almost always resulted in the loss of their land rights to large corporate owners, especially to the Southern Pacific Railroad, which by that time controlled a great proportion of California's land, and a greater proportion of her politicians.

The pernicious pattern of monopoly of the land expanded quickly during the years from 1890 to 1900, the percentage of tenant farmers growing to nearly 25 percent (Starr 1985). Economic and agricultural disasters bludgeoned California's growers, her wine industry, for example, having endured three cycles of boom and bust, widespread bankruptcy, and a disastrous Phylloxera epidemic by the closing decade of the nineteenth century. Agriculture had long since eclipsed mining as California's primary industry, and thus the 1890s were particularly grueling as first the wheat market crashed, then wool prices bottomed out. Her famous citrus industry not having yet come to full fruit, California's agricultural life was grim and repellant to settlers, offering as it did "long hours and a repetitive diet, ramshackle housing, few schools, inadequate medical care . . . A tough lonely life" (Starr 1985, 167).

Josiah Royce was a son of that land, his parents having settled as ranchers in Grass Valley, in northern California. For the sake of his future, the family moved to San Francisco so that Josiah could attend high school. Education suited him; he was among the University of California's first alumni (class of 1875). He returned from graduate studies at Johns Hopkins to accept an appointment at the University of California, where his tenure was much shorter than that of his predecessor, Professor Sill, but certainly no happier. His four years in the English Department saw him assigned "the irksome task of pounding principles of composition into freshmen" (Starr 1985, 150). Sighed Royce in a letter to a friend: "While Berkeley may claim to be the Athens of the Pacific, the Athens so far lacks its Pericles, its Socrates, its Phidias, in fact all its list of great names from Solon on. It also lacks wit and wisdom in the ranks of its common people" (Starr 1985, 150). In 1883 Royce ascended into Harvard and set about creating his masterwork, *The Problems of Christianity*.

Professor Bradley replaced Royce in the English Department and took to pounding those same principles of composition that had driven Royce to the problems of Christianity. For his syntax Bradley was appointed professor of rhetoric in 1895. He attained this position by virtue of his program of intense surveillance of students' errors. He maintained meticulous ledgers documenting each student's efforts—and missteps—on the daily themes that they wrote.[1] George Stewart, a professor in the English Department in years subsequent to Bradley's tenure, surveying some eight thousand of Bradley's ledger entries, confessed himself "appall[ed]" by their "compulsiveness" (Stewart 1968, 18). Benjamin Kurtz, a colleague of Bradley's in later years, shied away from talk of outright compulsion, characterizing Bradley as having a "clear, incisive, almost hypercritical mind" (Kurtz 1943, 120). This penchant for hypercriticism is reported in an anecdote by Walter Hart, a colleague of Bradley: Bicycling along San Pablo Avenue in 1899, Hart gestured past the nearly empty grasslands to the Berkeley Hills, where eucalyptus trees had recently been planted. "From a distance," Hart remarked, "they look like pines." "Yes," intoned Bradley, "They simulate the conifers" (Stewart 1968, 18).

Bradley introduced a freshman course in composition, English Prose Style, the required text for which was *Manual of English Prose Literature*, by William Minto. This book figures prominently in stories of student life in those early years. An annual event was the "Burial of Minto," when students gathered at a plot west of where the faculty club now sits to celebrate a mass interment of this textual reminder of their experiences with composition. In later years, as campus construction encroached upon the Minto Cemetery, the burial ceremony was replaced by a cremation, Mintos stacked upon a mighty pyre (Stewart 1968).

Bradley seemed not to have been burned in effigy during these rituals; indeed, he seemed never to have warmed to the students at all, at least to the composition students. In the first months of his first year at the University of California, Bradley notes in his diary: "January 15, 1883. Began freshman work. Several ne'er-do-wells eliminated."[2] But not all of them, apparently. A month into the semester, Bradley reports that he conferred with his chairman, A. S. Cook, later of Yale, on ways of "enforcing exactness."[3] From the very beginning of his tenure at the university, Bradley pursued a career in composition enforcement. His job as a parsekeeper is glaringly apparent in his diary entry concerning the administration of entrance examinations for the 1883–84 academic year: "Fifteen students fail the entrance examination in Subjects 1 and 14."[4] So closely trained were his eyes on the failures, as his compendious ledger of students' errors will later attest, Bradley neglected even to record the number of passing scores.

All was not lost for the fifteen failures, however. They were given a second chance to enter this cash-strapped young university the following January. Bradley doesn't record their results; perhaps in the absence of his notice of failure, we can infer passing scores. It is difficult, at any rate, not to infer that at least some of the luckless fifteen contributed to the sense of disgust he recorded in his diary a few days after the second exam: "Ceaseless interviews with the unfortunate, the lazy, and the feeble-minded."[5]

A year further into his service at the university, the disgust seems to have softened into dismay. The examinees for the year 1885–86 are merely "not a very well prepared lot."[6] By 1888 failure seems to have become the normal outcome: "Half of the students are conditioned."[7]

Altogether, much about Bradley's early years at UC seems to have contributed to his sense of dismay. In each of his diaries from 1884 through 1888, Bradley complains about Chairman Cook's repeated refusal to assign someone to help him with the burden of correcting freshman themes. In September of 1884, it seemed that a Mr. Vighte was poised to help Bradley with the themes, but Vighte abruptly resigned. Cook "wishes that there were more of the heroic in [Vighte]."[8] It is not clear whether Cook thinks that heroism is required to correct freshman themes, or to do so under Bradley's supervision. A later diary entry supports the latter interpretation. A Mr. Stoddard, who had been assisting Bradley, resigned in 1888. In an angry confrontation, the chairman accuses Bradley of "driving off Stoddard, a better man."[9]

Another failure with which Bradley had to struggle was the university's perennial refusal to grant him an increase in salary. His diaries for the years 1884 through 1888 record frequent conversations with Chairman Cook, each one ending in disappointment for Bradley. In fairness to both men, the possibility should be considered that it was neither Cook's parsimony nor Bradley's unsatisfactory job performance that prevented the salary increase. The university was profoundly ill-funded in those years. It was not until 1887 that the legislature voted for the university to receive the proceeds of a tax of one cent per one hundred dollars of property tax collected (Ferrier 1930).

The passage of this mil tax was historic in that it committed the legislature to the support of higher education. It is also of historic value to my story of the rhetoric of remediation at UC. In legislative hearings on this proposed tax, the issue of education standards was raised (perhaps for the first time in California's legislative history, but most certainly not for the last). This time, the complaint was that the University of California's standards were too high. Why should the state support the university, legislators asked, when instruction there aimed well over the heads of most of California's young citizens? In his response to the query, UC President Davis took a brilliant rhetorical turn on the floor of the statehouse. His first step was to convince the legislators that it wasn't that UC's standards were too high; it was that the high schools' ("feeder schools'") standards were too low. The university needed to expand the visitors' program and send more of its faculty out to the schools to supervise instruction and raise the quality of students' preparation. Such supervision, President Davis reminded the legislators, costs money.

Davis's second rhetorical step was more intricate. Not only are UC's standards low, he claimed, they're much lower than those of the eastern schools. And it is this deficiency, insisted Davis in 1888, that will make California suffer. Californians are plagued, he lamented, not because her young people can't get into higher education, but because higher education isn't *even harder* to get into. "The welfare of the whole community is ultimately involved in the maintenance of [UC's] standards," he claimed (Ferrier 1930, 378).

One could argue that this claim marks Davis as particularly forward thinking, almost prescient, in his vision of a California where vast numbers of her citizens receive postsecondary education, as is true today. That, however, was not the California that Davis resided in, nor the university that he presided over in 1887. In simple fact, President Davis's university educated 333 young persons that year, 1 University-of-California-trained student for every 2600 Californians. It's hard to imagine that such a ratio could have much impact on the welfare of the state. Nevertheless, the legislature found Davis's rhetoric compelling. He left Sacramento with the mil tax in his pocket.

In May of the same year, half of Professor Bradley's examinees in composition failed satisfactorily to analyze these lines from Shakespeare's *Julius Caesar*:[10]

> But 'tis a common proof
> That lowliness is young ambition's ladder
> Whereto the climber-upward turns his face;
> But when he once attains the upmost round
> He then unto the ladder turns his back,
> Looks into the clouds, scorning the base degrees
> By which he did ascend. (Act II, Scene 1, Lines 21–27)

President Davis's university had more than a few steps to go before it could attain the upmost round, but that climber-upward already had begun to scan the clouds. Davis's rhetorical triumph, then, can be seen as the precursor of Gayley's sleight-of-pen described in the previous chapter. It is certainly as brilliant as Gayley's, and arguably more valuable: while Professor Gayley's rhetoric bought respect among academics back East for a gawky young University of California, President Davis's rhetoric bought the state's continuing support. As rhetoricians, Gayley and Davis couldn't have been more different, nor could the assertions they put forward. However, there is a very important commonality about their tactics: both chose the same axis upon which to spin the University of California story—the deficiencies of her students. While Gayley's academic rhetoric marched solemnly to strains of "Pomp and Circumstance," President Davis's spin had a quirky jurisprudential elegance that only a legislator could love: The university needs money to elevate its curriculum because California's young people are too deficient to benefit from what the university has to offer at present, *and* they will be even more deficient once the university gets the money to raise its standards. The vigilance of people like the English Department's Professor Bradley will save California from herself. The remedial student is the problem to be solved; the welfare of the state depends on it. Or to put forward an assertion warranted by a hundred years of hindsight: the welfare of the university depends in no slight way upon the remedial student.

CHAPTER 3

"They Can Neither Read Nor Write"

[California and the Far West] is a rich and inexhaustible field over which the dawn of future commercial and industrial importance is just breaking.

Sunset Magazine, *vol. 1, no. 1, 1898 (Jaehn 1998, 82).*

[California and the Far West] was a region without precedent and with few certainties, struggling for idea and metaphor.

Kevin Starr (1998) on Sunset's *influence.*

IF HUBERT HOWE BANCROFT (188?) inaugurated California's image industry with his *Annals of the California Gold Era: 1848–1859* in the heady, brutal days of the gold rush, Southern Pacific's *Sunset Magazine* surely inherited the mantle of leadership in self-promotion, and set about praising rural life in California. Established in 1898 as an organ of the Southern Pacific Railroad, *Sunset* wordsmithed tirelessly to represent California as a desirable place for tourists, and "to encourage some passengers to settle down out West" (Starr 1998, 79).

Sunset's inducements may have been enough for the average settler, but Benjamin Ide Wheeler needed more reason to leave Cornell for the University of California, characterized in New York's *Utica Observer* in 1901 as "a weak institution, with plenty of land, a collection of broken-down buildings, beggarly endowments, and few students" (Douglass 2000, 100). Wheeler's acceptance of the presidency of the University of California in

1899 was contingent upon the regents' capitulation to three demands: that he alone be the means of communication between faculty and regents; that he alone have the authority to hire and fire faculty, and to set their salaries; and that the regents present to the faculty, and the public, a united front of support for Wheeler's decisions, regardless of their individual objections (Stadtman 1970, 181).

These stiff conditions bespeak a candidate very sure of his qualifications for the job. The regents' acceptance of them bespeaks a university weary of a succession of presidents and a run of ineffectual administrations.[1] The University of California was in fact something of a banana republic in those days, the regents having ushered in—and out—some eight presidents in thirty years, in contrast to Harvard's one president, Charles William Eliot, during that period, and Michigan's two (James Angell for twenty-eight of those thirty years).

Readers of the *Dial* in 1894 may have been urged to study carefully the University of California's scheme of instruction, so different from the common eastern type, but had they looked very closely, they would have seen that much of that instruction offered at this westernmost outpost of culture was taking place in tents. In the late 1890s, Regent Phoebe Apperson Hearst, chagrined that this city on a hill was something of a tent city, embarked upon her famous philanthropic project to erect some decent buildings, commission some civilizing statuary, and impart a little dignity to a university which, after all, bore Bishop Berkeley's burdensome exhortation "Westward the course of empire makes its way" (Stadtman 1970).

President Wheeler was well suited to make the University of California live up to this most imperial of expectations; he had an international reputation as a Heidelberg-trained scholar of classical philology ("a philologist who outgrew philology" [Slosson 1910, 155]), and an impressive network of friends, including then-former President Grover Cleveland and then-future President Theodore Roosevelt. And—no insignificant detail for rugged Californians—he'd been a star athlete in his undergraduate days at Brown. Wheeler was known for his decisiveness, if not for his tact, and he spoke unhesitatingly of the "promise and backwardness of California" (Starr 1985, 66). He demanded that the University of California abandon its insularity and become a "world university." California's university, insisted Wheeler, "dare not be in any sense provincial" (Ferrier 1930, 398).

Speaking at Wheeler's inauguration, Stanford President David Starr Jordan insisted that it was the duty of a university president to "set the university's pace, frame its ideals, and choose its men in whom his ideals can be realized" (Miller 1979, 32). One of the men Wheeler chose to realize his ideals was Chauncey Wetmore Wells. A Yale man,[2] Wells joined the English Department as professor of English Composition. Like Professor Bradley, Wells found his students disappointing. In his introduction to *A Book of Prose Narratives*, an anthology he collected for freshmen, Wells sighs, "One great difficulty we all must meet is in teaching our students, especially the freshmen, to write plainly and sensibly" (Wells 1914, iii). This followed the more immediate disappointment that is said to have befallen him in 1901, when he and his wife gazed upon the young University of California for the first time. Stepping gingerly off the steam train that in those days ran up Shattuck Avenue, they looked across the hay fields to the university's few dreary buildings, linked by dusty dirt paths. Apropos of his new academic appointment, Wells turned to his wife and said, "Mary, somebody has been pulling our leg" (Stewart 1968, 20).

His appointment was, of course, no joke. President Benjamin Wheeler had great plans for the growth and development of the University of California. A colleague remembers the Wheeler era thus: "The University during those days [1899–1918] was in the process of changing from a college to a university, from teaching to research. This change was the task of Wheeler, and in it he could be somewhat ruthless."[3]

These were ruthless times in California, not that the sunny republic had heretofore been particularly ruthful. By this time, though, the frontier had been closed, the boom-and-bust volubility had subsided, and the six-shooters had been holstered. It was no longer greed and the expectation of striking gold that held Californians hostage. Rather it was the iron clutch of the Southern Pacific Railroad, and the drive to empire of the Big Four,[4] who engineered the railroad's phenomenal control over California's economic, and thus social, well-being. Simply put, the Southern Pacific Railroad owned California at the end of the century.

Historians have suggested that during this period California stood in a colonial relationship to the eastern states. Less than 5 percent of California's industrial output was in manufactured goods; the rest of her needs she imported from back East. The bulk of California's wealth lay in her extractive industries—timber, petroleum, and minerals—and in her agriculture (Malone and Etulain 1989). By the early years of the twentieth century, California's agricultural exports were beginning to grace tables throughout America. Her olives, apricots, almonds, walnuts, dates, and plums soon dominated the national market. Oranges, peaches, pears, raisins, nectarines, and figs followed (Starr 1985). Ice-cooled railcars were perfected, and lettuce, tomatoes, spinach, cucumber, chard, eggplant, asparagus, and even artichokes rode the rails, bringing California fame and bringing the Southern Pacific Railroad fortune.

In addition to controlling 10 million acres of California land, including some $15 million worth of oil fields—a grant from the federal government —the Southern Pacific controlled the transport of almost every bushel of California's agricultural products. Of course, transportation systems, particularly ones so fundamental to the public good, are subject to legislative and judicial control. To that end, the Southern Pacific had long been in the business of controlling California's public servants. Governor Gage's election, in 1898; Governor Pardee's, in 1902; and Governor Gillett's, in 1906, were all left to the capable, and very busy, hands of William F. Herrin, Director of Southern Pacific's Political Bureau (Mowry 1951). Indeed, the Southern Pacific's Political Bureau was said to have written Governor Pardee's platform. The Southern Pacific Railroad controlled legislators at the state and federal level,[5] members of the local judiciary, some of San Francisco's city supervisors, and was strongly believed to have bought itself a federal judge (Mowry 1951).[6] This political machine was at least as well oiled and maintained as the railroad itself, and it delivered the goods every bit as efficiently.

Kickbacks, corruption, and patronage work only when they are distributed widely enough to squelch disquiet. This happened in California during the flush years when "the entire state seemed to move on the lubricant of graft and privilege" (Mowry 1951, 13). However, during the lean years, as for example, the Panic of 1893 and its aftermath throughout the remainder of the decade and into the beginning of the new century, Californians became restive, resentful of the Southern Pacific's immense power.

In 1897 James D. Phelan was elected mayor of San Francisco on an anti-Southern Pacific platform. He promised city ownership of street railways, water, gas, and electricity.[7] His administration saw the first of a series of labor disputes, each one met with heavy police action. The general strike in San Francisco in 1901 brought the city to a standstill. Sixty percent of city businesses were closed as more than twenty-two unions struck for improved working conditions and wages (Starr 1985, 33). Employers brought in strikebreakers and a small army of private strike police, with Mayor Phelan's complicity, if not actual blessing. The unions admitted defeat and Southern Pacific's Governor Gage engineered a humiliating back-to-work agreement.

Professor Chauncey Wetmore Wells and his wife Mary were fortunate enough not to have arrived in San Francisco during the melee of the general strike, and thus were able to sail across the Bay and make their way up Shattuck Avenue on the steam train without incident. Although they didn't climb huffily back on that train, they were not of a mind to celebrate their good fortune at having arrived at the University of California uninjured. Wells's pride suffered a great blow that day when he beheld his professional future, and he never really recovered. He stayed for what a biographer characterized as a life of "academic defeat" (Stewart 1968, 21).

In Wells's mind, University of California's President Wheeler bore much of the blame for this defeat. Wheeler had called Wells west with the implied promise that he would head his own department of composition, but this never transpired.[8] In his time Wheeler established twenty new departments, but a department of composition was not among them. Late in his career, Wells remarked to a colleague in English, "Wheeler thought he wanted a composition mill, but he lost interest in it later" (Stewart 1968, 21). Wells suffered another disappointment at Wheeler's hands: he had been granted a sabbatical to study the University of Missouri's newly established School of Journalism, and to bring back a curricular plan for a department of journalism for the University of California, presumably under his—Wells's—direction. Upon his return Wells gained an audience with Wheeler and presented his plan, only to realize that Wheeler had moved on in his thinking. "We don't want a Department of Journalism," he snorted. "Let Stanford do that!"[9] Wells went back to the classroom and to his career of making freshmen write plainly and sensibly.

It is not clear whether Wells was correct in laying his disappointments at Wheeler's door. Nothing in Wheeler's papers indicates that he ever communicated to Wells, or to others, the desire to have a department of journalism or a department of composition, although the notion of a "composition mill," if a bit coarse, would seem to accord with Wheeler's general mistrust of the English Department and its work. He regarded literature in English as something that anyone could read unaided. Classroom instruction in English literature he saw as dilettantish, at best. Stewart reports Wheeler as convinced that the English Department could do its best service by teaching elementary composition. "And," Wheeler added testily, "you do not need high-paid full professors to do that" (1968, 28).[10] He might well have been thinking of Charles Mills Gayley, who earned at Berkeley twice the salary he'd commanded at the University of Michigan.

By 1899, President Wheeler's inaugural year, Gayley had been running the English Department for a decade. He had been called to the University of California because the English Department was said to need a "wide-awake scholar" (Kurtz 1943, 93), and he was that. His classes were popular, and difficult. (A prewritten essay for one of Gayley's courses cost five dollars, while an essay for any other course fetched fifty cents [Kurtz 1943, 87]). His course entitled "Oral Debates on Literary Topics" played to a standing-room-only crowd of male students only (the better to impart a "lifelong, masculine interest in literature" [Kurtz 1943, 11]).

Similarly, Gayley's Great Books course, inaugurated during Wheeler's second year in office, was a massive success, attracting students not just from the English Department, but from throughout the university, including the colleges of Commerce and Applied Sciences.[11] Townspeople began attending these lectures, and the course was moved to increasingly larger venues until it finally reached the Greek Theatre in 1909, where Gayley was said to have lectured on Great Books to audiences of over one thousand. President Wheeler, however, was not impressed either by the size of Gayley's following or the quality of his lectures. He once referred to it as "the course in which Gayley made little books out of Great Books" (Kurtz 1943, 153).

Gayley was the son of English parents who emigrated to the United States when he was quite young; his biographer describes him as "vaguely British" (Kurtz 1943, 87). He had been trained at Oxford, and his idea of a university was very much as a locus for the transmission of the classical tradition. Gayley had proposed to outgoing President Martin Kellogg that the University of California establish a student society and debating club along the lines of the Oxford Union.[12] Kellogg endorsed the proposal and it met favor among the regents. However, when President Wheeler assumed office, the proposal died abruptly. Wheeler had no time for re-creating English collegiate life at his university.

Wheeler was intent upon implanting a German-style research university on California's coast, and the English Department, however vital to the life of undergraduates, did not contribute to that vision. Rather, Wheeler's fierce energies were trained elsewhere—for example, on the founding of the Political Science and Economics departments. And his philological impulse was directed toward the development of the Spanish Department.[13] The American university had already begun the momentous process of differentiating into departments, and of undertaking a research mission (Veysey 1965), and Wheeler had to hustle to move his University of California into her place in the sun.

It must be admitted that the sun shone substantially brighter down the peninsula. Stanford University had opened in 1891, with the largest endowment of any American university of the time ($30 million) and a much bigger enrollment in its first year than UC had in its twenty-second year. The University of California was cast immediately into the shadow of her well-heeled cousin. Stanford President David Starr Jordan was seen as California's leading intellectual, easily eclipsing anyone the University of California had on offer.

In 1899, the year Wheeler took the reins of the university, the California legislature voted Stanford into quasi-public status. John Swett, in *Public Education in California* (1911) described Stanford's situation thus: "Though not under direct state control [Stanford] fulfills many functions of a state university. It is open to both men and women; it has no tuition fees, it has a pedagogy department for the training of teachers, it has the elective system in studies" (267). In his 1910 study *Great American Universities*, Edwin Slosson commented that friends of the University of California "felt some apprehension of the effect of the founding of Stanford" (1910, 163). And it is no wonder, Slosson reflected, considering the University of California's "receiving insufficient support from the State, [being] forced to do much work of high school grade, having only a few hundred students with its buildings getting old and shabby, and little prospect of getting better ones" (163). If the University of California really was to be the institution "where a man could look in the face the 19th century" (Barth 1994, 33), it would need a makeover, and Wheeler's model would be the German-style research institution, first domesticated at Johns Hopkins.

By Wheeler's lights, Gayley's English Department had nothing to contribute to that makeover. Thus, despite accelerating rates of enrollment and increasing demand for access to higher education—or perhaps because of this—the English Department during the Wheeler era remained an instructional unit where "freshman work in English was signally emphasized and developed" (Kurtz 1943, 157).

This signal emphasis on freshman work was not surprising; when Wheeler took over the university, the freshman class was twice the size of the senior class (May 1993). As Wheeler moaned early in his administration, "The students are coming down like an avalanche."[14] Wheeler's job was to deflect that avalanche, to prevent the crush of students from burying the University of California in mediocrity. He had to sustain an elegant balance: he was responsible to the taxpayers to educate the growing numbers of qualified young Californians that the high schools sent to him, but he was responsible also to build the university's prestige, to craft the University of California into a "world university" (Ferrier 1930, 398).

One of the people who could help Wheeler maintain the balance sheet was Chauncey Wetmore Wells. As professor of composition (though never chair of that elusive department of composition), Wells administered the Subject A examination to those freshmen. Poor performance on the exam, it will be remembered, did not bar a student from entering the University of California. It merely marked him or her as not yet up to the university's exacting standards. The student was "conditioned" in composition, and subjected to a program of surveillance by the Special Committee on the Treatment of Incompetent Students, chaired by Alexis Lange, then professor of English, later head of the Education Department (Stewart 1968).

1902 was the first year that Wells administered the Subject A examination, and it was the first time since the establishment of the exam in 1883 that students wrote to a new topic. Before Wells, students had been asked to summarize for the examiner some aspect of their exposure in high school to English literature, as for example:

> Give a clear and orderly account of your training in English and your estimation of what it has accomplished for you. (Johnson 1941, 293)

These topics frequently resulted in students' labored comments on Lowell's "The Vision of Sir Launfal" or Scott's "The Lay of the Last Minstrel," both popular among the works listed by Gayley and Bradley (1894) in their *Suggestions to High School Teachers of English in the Secondary Schools*. They yielded a failure rate of approximately 50 percent. Wells, mindful perhaps, of President Wheeler's injunction that the University of California "dare not be provincial," administered an exam that was less bookish and more worldly:

> Give a clear and succinct sketch, as if for a newspaper, of the rise and development of a recent affair—for example, the Venezuela Affair, Canal Treaty, Peary Expedition, Warner Ranch Indians, Irrigation of Arid Lands. (Johnson 1934, 294)

Curiously, students writing to this new topic failed at the same rate—50 percent—confounding the commonsense notion that a recap of a current event much discussed in the press would offer examinees—and readers—a more engrossing and productive experience than dutiful remarks on Sir Launfal might elicit. These 50 percent entered the university, just as their better half did, but they were declared incompetent and remanded to Professor Lange's committee for surveillance (Kurtz 1943).

Again, these "incompetents" did important work for the university. They were the vehicle through which the University of California could advertise its strict standards—after all, 50 percent of examinees were shown to be not up to UC-quality work. But incompetence was only to be remarked upon publicly, and was not to be a bar to admission. Thus, enrollment figures were robust (2248 undergraduate students in 1902). Californians could be reassured that their university was meeting the growing demand for higher education, and at the same time be reassured that their university upheld high standards.

Beginning in 1902, an "incompetent" had some actual classroom work —and not just symbolic work—to do. If he was a student in the College of Mechanics and Mining, or in Civil Engineering, he was required to enroll in English 3A: Practical Composition, a course on writing abstracts and reports, exposition and description, and business correspondence.[15] The following year, specific remedies for the failing 50 percent expanded into other departments. If a conditioned student was enrolled in the Colleges of Letters, Social Sciences, or Natural Sciences, he or she had to take English A, a course "designed for those whose preparation for more advanced writing is insufficient."[16] In contrast to the practical approach of English 3A, this new course followed a more belletristic route: after sentence-level drills, the course moved to "the study of such prose masterpieces as meet the needs of the class."[17]

In 1904, Gayley and Bradley published the second edition of their influential booklet, *Suggestions for Teachers of English in the Secondary Schools*. Its influence was disproportionate to its size (a mere seventy-eight pages); Benjamin Kurtz, Gayley's biographer, described it as the "chief *vade mecum* of the English teachers in the State" (1943, 133). The booklet began, as had the first edition, with a complaint: "Attention has been directed of late to the lamentable condition of English instruction in the secondary schools" (Gayley and Bradley 1904, 2). In the years since the publication and wide distribution of the first edition of *Suggestions*, little seemed to have changed in the high schools. Gayley and Bradley found that "[t]he most common form of deficiency of students who apply to a university—and not a few of them actually get in—is that they can neither read nor write" (26).

Not a few of them actually got in again in 1904. Of the freshmen accepted that year, some 50 percent had failed to acquit themselves to the satisfaction of the Subject A Examiners. That year the topics had promised to be more accessible than ever; students could choose from, among others, the following:

> My Impressions of Berkeley
> My School
> My Choice of College (e.g., Letters and Science, Social Science)
> The Rains of Last March (Johnson 1934, 294)

1905 saw a sea change in the Subject A exam. Enrollment at the university was 2519, approximately a 40 percent increase since Wheeler had taken over the presidency of the University of California six years previously. Many more high schools had been accredited, and the university felt, as perhaps never before, its duty to serve the needs of the taxpayers.

Examinees in 1905 had to write three papers, each one a significant departure from the traditional emphasis on literary themes. This exam gave students considerable scope to display their expository skills in a range of subjects.

Paper 1 drew on students' knowledge of history, natural history, or literature:

> Write a brief biographical paper on some American statesman with an estimation of the significance of his work in our national development.
>
> Describe the conditions leading up to the War of the American Revolution.
>
> Present a generalized view of a California winter. (Johnson 1934, 295)

Paper 2 drew on students' knowledge of science or math:

> State the composition of the atmosphere, and describe experiments that prove your statements.
>
> Describe the changes produced in some substance, such as ice, by the continuous application of heat.
>
> Describe the construction of some electrical contrivance—such as a battery, telephone, induction coil, electromagnet, or galvanometer—and state the general physical principle upon which its operation depends.
>
> Given two equations of the first degree, state in logical order and in general language the steps necessary to determine the values of the two unknown quantities. (Johnson 1934, 295)

Finally, Paper 3 called on students to respond to a reading passage from Macaulay's *History of English Civilization* by commenting on the proposition that "the progress of civilization has diminished the comforts of a portion of the poorest class" (Johnson 1934, 295).

Papers 1 and 2 came with the proviso that "the papers will be rated not so much on accuracy of knowledge involved as upon organization of thought and effectiveness of expression" (Johnson 1934, 295). The record of that year's exam administration, unfortunately, includes no discussion of the difficulties that these new topics might have posed for examinees, or indeed for readers. No information is given as to the relative weight accorded each paper; whether the discussion, e.g., of a galvanometer, offered each young writer adequate scope to display his or her ability "to write correctly, clearly, and pertinently on all the lines on which his thought is exercised" as the university expected its entrants to do.[18] Neither does the record indicate whether or not the examiners found it possible to over-look inaccuracies of content, as they promised to do. The record merely indicates the depressing, but by now wholly predictable, recurrence of the 50 percent failure rate.

As befits an administrator facing an avalanche, Wheeler is widely re-ported to have demanded a toughening of standards. In 1907 he insisted that the newly formed Committee on Subject A implement and publicize a new standard: students would not be admitted to upper-division stand-ing, and would thus be ineligible for a Junior Certificate, until they had passed the Subject A exam, or otherwise satisfied the committee as to their writing proficiency.[19] There is no indication in the available minutes of the Committee on the Treatment of Incompetent Students or the Committee on Subject A that students were dismissed for failing to demonstrate writing proficiency by their junior years. The only evidence that these standards had an effect was Gayley's request in 1892 that two students be placed on "limited student" status because of the "deficiency of their themes."[20] The more important effect of this new "standard" was rhetorical: it preserved the University of California's claim to exclusivity while still accommodating the avalanche.

In 1913, a more pragmatic accommodation was suggested. The Com-mittee on Subject A proposed that the English Department establish a course in English composition for those students who failed the exam. The course was to be taught by students from the Student Teachers' Course in the Education Department. They would receive no pay for this work, but it would substitute for the practice teaching required of candidates for the high school teaching certificate. The Committee on Subject A would judge papers written during this course in lieu of a final Subject A exam.[21]

Gayley and Wells objected to a vote on this motion, claiming that "the English department does not feel authorized to make any recommenda-tion,"[22] and the motion died. It was not until 1916 that it was resurrected, this time as a proposal crafted by the English Department itself, and pre-sented by Professor Kurtz, with instruction to be in the hands of a "paid officer," a member of the English Department faculty. This time, the pro-posal succeeded. Students got a course in Subject A, and the university got an avenue through which it could distinguish itself as a worthy insti-tution. Professor Kurtz's rhetoric in justifying the need for this instruction is in itself instructive: "The problem" he urged, "is that the student is constantly subjected to unedifying influences of myriad examples of poor English."[23] This is an assertion that likely would have fallen on receptive ears in those years when immigration and in-migration to California was robust. In fact, among the Subject A exam topics for 1914 was the question "Should there be a literacy test for immigrants?" (Johnson 1934, 296).

Wheeler was widely reported to have demanded a tightening of standards in these early years of the new century (Kurtz 1943; Slosson 1910; Ferrier 1930). Such reports always bid fair to raise an institution's status in the public eye. However, a closer consideration of the actual changes in requirements paints a different picture. In 1899, the standards that Wheeler inherited from his predecessor mandated the following graduation requirements for students in the College of Liberal Culture (comprising the College of Letters, College of Social Sciences, and College of Natural Sciences):

65 hours in prescribed studies (e.g., English, math, language ancient or modern, military studies)

+ 30 hours "group electives" (chosen from such groups as history, philosophy, or pedagogy)

+ 30 hours free electives

= 125 unit hours total (Conmy 1928, 279)

By 1905–06, six years into Wheeler's administration, amidst much public comment about the raising of standards, the following graduation requirements obtained in the College of Liberal Culture:

64 unit hours in prescribed studies (to be completed by the end of junior year)

+ 24 unit hours in one major department

+ 36 unit hours free electives

= 124 unit hours total (Conmy 1928, 283)

Thus a new calculus was advanced, one that reduced the unit hours of prescribed studies, increased the unit hours of free electives, and lowered by one unit hour the coursework required for graduation. Rather more an exercise in math than an effort to raise standards, it did the trick: the avalanche was accommodated. Wheeler's rhetorical turn was more mathematical than President Davis's in 1887, but at least as efficacious. These students were neither lost to Stanford, nor sent back home to their taxpaying parents. The University of California was widely said to have raised its standards.

Wheeler's era coincided very consequently with California's Progressive Era, roughly 1900–20, and, without detracting from his very great powers as an educational empire builder, it is fair to say that the University of California's growth during those years was fueled by a strong legislative will to reform the citizen's relationship to the state. In California, the Progressive movement gathered its strength as a response from outraged citizenry to years of corrupt governance and the iron control of the Southern Pacific Railroad.

California Progressivism stood for the regulation of public utilities, particularly for curtailment of the Southern Pacific's powers; for tax reform; for electoral refinements intended to place more power in the voters' hands, such as the initiative, referendum, and recall; for cross-filing of candidates (a practice that enabled candidates to run in other parties' primaries); for bank reforms; for women's suffrage; and for a comprehensive system of public education. The Progressive movement gave political voice to the apprehension that industrialism had grievously frayed the fabric of American life. This idea carried particular weight for California in those years when the state's value to the nation lay in her extractive industries. Further, and importantly for the health and prosperity of the University of California, the Progressive movement drew power from dressing its rhetoric in the intellectual fashion of the day, characterizing as "evolutionary" (and therewith wrapping in the saving mantle of science) all aspects of social change.

Progressives, then, were matchmakers in the marriage of scientism and industrialism. The role of the university in this match was crucial. Principles of scientific management were to be applied to all aspects of the Industrial Age, the end goal being the vast improvement of social mobility. Public education was to provide nothing less than "a ladder from the gutter to the university" (Douglass 2000, 71).

California's Progressive expectations of higher education drew deeply from the example set by the University of Wisconsin during Governor Robert Lafollette's administration. Lafollette saw that the state university should "minister in a direct and practical way to the material interests of the state" (Curtis and Carstensen 1949, 90). Progressive John Randolph Haynes advised California Governor Hiram Johnson that the role of higher education was to create new leaders for the new ways of conducting business, government, and industry. The university's duty, he insisted, was "to organize the energies of our scientists, our physicists, chemists, machinists, into armies of research."[24] The energies of teachers were to be professionalized, specialized. Schools were to be transformed to meet the evolutionary needs of a new industrial age. The Progressive movement was shot through with the notion of evolution. David Starr Jordan, writing in *Popular Science Monthly* in 1903, saw public education from elementary school to the university as "the key to America's evolving social and moral experiment" (143).

By 1909, enrollment at the University of California had risen to 2953. Wheeler got the legislature to approve a second mil tax, but the very next year the university lost this source of state funding. Progressive Governor Johnson had been swept into office in 1910 on an anti-corruption, anti–Southern Pacific Railroad, clean-government platform. One of Johnson's first congressional coups was a broad tax reform that took property tax payments out of state coffers and redirected them to the cities and counties. This legislation vitiated the university's block allocation budget.

Johnson was a great friend of higher education, however, and he was eager to accept Wheeler's advice and to propose a "state university fund." The University of California henceforth was to draw its budget from California's general fund, on a per-capita or per-student basis. Before this, funding had not been tied to enrollment. This enrollment-based funding program carried an annual 7 percent increase, as that had been the average growth in the student body in each of the previous three years. Enrollment-based funding served the university well in those first few years of Johnson's administration. Wheeler was able to continue his ambitious program of hiring new faculty and creating and expanding departments. Enrollment-based funding gave the university a clear fiscal motive for welcoming new students. Enrollment growth, however, soon surpassed 7 percent per annum, and this led, once again, to a crisis in funding. The 7 percent allocation was soon recalibrated upward, and that brought slight, but only slight, relief. The University of California continued to feel the tensions—economic as well as social—of increasing demands for access to higher education.

CHAPTER 4

"Beautiful but Dumb"

> Some of our students are as brilliant and as
> ambitious as any scholar of medieval times.
> Some have the mind but little desire to use
> it. Some are beautiful but dumb, and some
> are not even beautiful. But we try to educate
> them all by similar means—an unattainable
> purpose.
>
> Robert Gordon Sproul, Address to the Common-
> wealth Club of California, July 25, 1930 (Pettitt
> 1966, 185).

ROBERT GORDON SPROUL took over the presidency of the University of
California at the beginning of the Great Depression. California's economic health was already in weakened condition, and had been for some
years, before the crash of October 24, 1929, so the shock waves from that
economic implosion hit the state hard.

In the 1930s, California still derived most of her wealth from agriculture. Then, as now, her agriculture was large scale, dependent on heavy
capital investment, and burdened with high operating costs. At that time,
some 60 percent of California's agricultural land was owned by 2 percent
of her farmers (Beck and Williams 1972, 392). California's agriculture was
dependent, as well, upon armies of migrant laborers, and as the Depression deepened on the Plains, migration to California intensified. In the
first few years of that grim decade, some 300,000 agricultural laborers
worked these "factories in the field" (McWilliams 1970), most of them in-

migrants, "tractored-out" from dustbowl states, all of them laboring under appalling conditions, scrabbling for pitiful wages. By 1933 the prevailing wage had dropped 50 percent (Starr 1996, 67). By the second half of the decade, some 350,000 workers had migrated from the Plains, driven by desperation and by the exploitive inducements of growers' representatives. Wages for agricultural workers, already depressed, dived to new depths of "sub-subsistence" (Starr 1996, 67). Not surprisingly, such conditions spawned bitter labor strife throughout the golden land.

The decade saw huge strikes in California's fields and canneries, as well as a massive—and bloody—police response. The 1933 strike of cotton pickers in the San Joaquin Valley saw eighteen thousand strikers brutally subdued, either forced back into the fields or arrested under the new strikebreaking Criminal Syndicalism Act. In 1934, striking apple pickers in Santa Rosa were beaten or burned back to their jobs (Beck and Williams 1972). Growers not only raised vigilante squads, they raised the specter of Communism. "Reds" were reported to be marching on Sacramento from various strike sites. "Minute Men to Fight Reds" shrieked a *San Francisco Examiner* headline on December 7, 1932, describing a standoff between a grower's private militia and striking workers (Starr 1996, 72).

The Communist threat arose again in May of 1934 in the massive waterfront strike that closed San Francisco's Embarcadero, and indeed all West Coast ports from Seattle to San Diego. The longshoremen's demand for a wage of one dollar a day quickly drew the support of other maritime unions, including the radio operators, seamen, and engineers. Describing the strike as "an insurrection which will lead to a civil war" (Beck and Williams 1972, 397), Governor Frank Merriam called in the National Guard. The Battle of Rincon Hill, waged on July 9, 1934, claimed the lives of 2 strikers and sent 266 more to hospital.

In 1936, strikers in Salinas's lettuce fields bore the organized ire of the police, the highway patrol, the American Legionnaires, and the growers' armies of hired muscle. California bled throughout the decade. Some six hundred thousand weary souls came to her for work, for food, for relief. Conservative Republican Governor James Rolph, elected in 1931, reacted to what he called "California's cataclysmic deficit" of $42 million by cutting her budget to the bone.

This was, of course, a wretched time to be responsible for the survival of a costly public institution dependent on the political will of a skeptical legislature, but Sproul was the University of California's best hope. His experience as university comptroller under President Barrows, and as vice president of business under President Campbell, had brought him before the legislature frequently to defend the university's budget. California lawmakers had long harbored reservations about the University of California's ability to provide the right kind of higher education for the state's young people, and the university had fought off a number of challenges from legislators and governors convinced that it was disserving California's agricultural interests. In its earliest years, the University of California had withstood the Grangers' challenge to the type of higher education a state university should provide. In 1921, the university met—and defeated —a legislative putsch to revoke its status as a land grant college and to divert those Morrill Act resources to the establishment of an independent state college of agriculture.

By 1930, skepticism in Sacramento had grown and taken root beyond the state's agricultural sector. Hard-pressed legislators were more disinclined than ever to fund the kind of higher education that the University of California stood for. The university was widely perceived as "elitist," unwilling to meet the needs of California's young people for practical higher education, and, importantly, unwilling to admit other institutions into the arena (Douglass 2000).

Throughout the early 1930s, the legislature was awash in bills to convert private four-year colleges and public two-year colleges into four-year regional colleges. The first proposal, in 1930, was for the allocation of three hundred thousand dollars to finance the upward expansion of Sacramento Junior College. Similar proposals from Fresno, San Jose, San Diego, and Redding followed in 1931 (Douglass 2000, 145). The University of California fought hard and defeated all these bills. President Sproul's strategy in this campaign to hold onto the university's unique status was to champion the role of the state's junior colleges. In the *Junior College Journal*, Sproul (1931) argued that "[t]he American creed that every human being shall have the opportunity for the utmost development of his chance to do the best he can does not mean that everyone must be admitted to a college or university within a few blocks of his home" (276). Sproul managed for a time to hold back the demand for expanded access to four-year colleges, but only at the cost of a growing public resentment against the university's monopoly on higher education. In its March 8, 1935 edition, the *Sacramento*

Bee complained of the University of California's "enormous appetite" for money, as well as the regents' evident plan "to throttle any educational progress in the State outside the reach of its domineering influence" (Douglass 2000, 158).

The move to expand higher education during an intense and prolonged period of economic distress like the Depression makes for a certain logic. The development of a regional college would stimulate employment for the region, and it would enable local students to live at home while receiving training for the careers that would surely open up when the economy recovered. In the same way that the land grant bailed out failing private colleges throughout the nation in the depression of the 1890s, and seeded state universities, it was hoped that expansion of public higher education in the Great Depression would hasten California's recovery, particularly in her hard-hit agricultural regions, and would open the door to higher education for more young Californians than the University of California alone could hope to do.

Such mass education was just the thing that Robert Sproul did not want. He repeatedly remarked that it was his responsibility "to avoid the open-door approach of most other Land Grant institutions" (Pettitt 1966, 2). His inaugural address in 1930 argued passionately that "there must be but one state university" (Pettitt 1966, 35). He took the occasion of his first Charter Day speech in 1931 to rally alumni against the regional college movement, urging as follows:

> Let us see that it [the university] meets the cultural demands of all, or at any rate all the important groups in the Commonwealth, but let us not exchange it for a collection of little replicas responding to purely local needs.[1]

Sproul's fight against "little replicas" led him to launch a media campaign of remarkable magnitude for the era, speaking on radio, giving newspaper interviews, and addressing public gatherings about the threat to public higher education that regional colleges constituted. Proponents of the regional college movement responded by scorning the University of California "monopoly" and characterizing Sproul as "selfish and shortsighted, attempting to shut out all other institutions from the benefits of state appropriations except the University of California and its little brother in Los Angeles" (Stadtman 1970, 66).

The legislature appointed, in 1930, a blue ribbon commission to study the "educational, geographic, financial, and organizational problems of public education" (Douglass 2000, 143). The commission found very substantial problems with the University of California. Foremost was their complaint that the university exercised undue control over secondary schooling. Specifically, from its earliest days the university had exercised authority to accredit high schools, and from Progressive days, accreditation had been a prerequisite for certain levels of funding for high schools. This resulted in the university effectively dictating that college-preparatory instruction be offered to high school students, whether or not they were college bound (Douglass 2000, 143). In the face of the Depression and the corollary unemployability of many high school graduates, the university's curricular control of the high schools seemed especially untenable to the committee: "It is unjust to handicap the many students who must prepare for their life work outside of the colleges."[2]

Upton Sinclair (1923), fiercest of critics and candidate for governor on the End Poverty in California (EPIC) ticket in 1933, had more to say about the University of California's hegemony over education:

> High above the city of Berkeley stands the University of California, a medieval fortress from which the intellectual life of the state is dominated and here we also find one of the grand dukes of the plutocracy in charge—[Regent] William H. Crocker. (127)

The University of California was, not surprisingly, horrified by Sinclair's candidacy. His defeat, and the inauguration of Robert Merriam, came as a relief, but not a respite from its budget worries. Governor-elect Merriam, while not hostile to the university, was unable to offer budget increases.

California's, and thus the University of California's, grave budget crisis strengthened Sproul's faith in the one-university doctrine. His opposition to four-year regional colleges led him to espouse the state's public junior colleges. California's junior college movement had begun in 1905, and in 1907, she had the nation's first junior college system. By the early 1930s there were some forty junior colleges throughout California (Douglass 2000). Junior colleges were not a threat to the university's source of appropriations because they drew their funding from local—and not state—revenues. They did not compete in the legislature for the higher education dollar. This important structural feature made them a vastly more attractive alternative to the proposed regional colleges that would have to get their funding from the same source as the university did: the legislature. Sproul was assiduous in his support of junior colleges, and he managed in 1931 to extract from their leadership, the Federation of Junior Colleges, the pledge to oppose any upward expansion of their institutions into four-year colleges (Stadtman 1970). In the face of local pressure on these institutions to expand, Sproul's securing such an assurance was a coup, demonstrating once again his very considerable persuasive talents.

The one-university doctrine was, however, a politically unsuitable response to the exigencies of the Great Depression and the rising expectation that public institutions, particularly public education, should solve California's serious economic problems. Despite Sproul's massive efforts, the damning findings of the blue ribbon commission continued to reverberate in the legislature and the press. Scrambling to recover from this blow, Sproul called for a second study, by an independent agency, and prevailed on the legislature to authorize the Carnegie Foundation for the Advancement of Teaching to study the structure of California's higher education under the direction of Henry Suzzallo, the foundation's president (Douglass 2000). This report, issued in 1932, was much more favorable to the university's interests. It called for the legislature to support only the University of California (at Berkeley and Los Angeles) "until they are saturated [in enrollment] and California is sufficiently prosperous" (Suzzallo 1932, 47). The Suzzallo report condemned the ongoing conversion of teachers' colleges into four-year liberal arts colleges, and it recommended that the university control all institutions of higher education established in the state above the junior college level: "The effort to get the Legislature to establish such senior colleges apart from University management and under the control of the State Boards, operating locally, is something to which the State should never consent" (Suzzallo 1932, 47).

Notwithstanding the prestige of the Carnegie Foundation, this report fell on deaf ears in the legislature. The movement to convert teachers' colleges into four-year regional colleges (usually by the simple expedient of deleting the graduation requirement of twelve units of education credits) gathered strength.[3] Communities continued to pressure their local junior colleges to expand upward. Sproul predicted despairingly that higher education in California "will face the certainty of mediocrity and the possibility of bankruptcy" (Stadtman 1970, 265).

Bankruptcy was, of course, a very real possibility in those years of the Depression, even without competition for the higher education dollar from the regional colleges. In the first half of that troubled decade, state appropriations to the university dropped precipitously, forcing Sproul to request of departments "a most exigent economy."[4] Austerity measures included a salary freeze, a hiring freeze, a reduction in the number of classes offered, an increase in class size,[5] a moratorium on all building projects (except the federally funded Crocker Radiation Laboratory), and cessation of any but the most essential maintenance (Pettitt 1966).

The only cost-cutting measure that Sproul could *not* afford to take was a reduction in enrollment. As a matter of fact, enrollment increased dramatically. Although the legislature's appropriations to UC dropped by 26 percent during the years 1931–39, Sproul permitted enrollment to rise by 25 percent (Douglass 2000, 140). He could hardly do otherwise. Sproul was in a bind. He was bound to find space for all the qualified students pounding at the gates of his university, regardless of the economic hardship their numbers presented. He had committed his presidency to the proposition that there could be but one state institution of higher education, the University of California. California did not need "little replicas" of universities scattered about the state, he argued passionately, and, in fact, their very existence would lower the impressive standards for higher education that the university had striven so hard to attain for California.

As ever, the matter of the University of California's standards was the awkward bit. From the first day of his presidency, Sproul countered the charge that the university's standards had been adjusted upward so as to cut out qualified students and control the enrollment surge. He insisted that the university was a "genuinely democratic institution."[6] Sproul, like President Davis in 1887, argued to all who would listen that UC's maintenance of high, exclusivist standards was *a service* to Californians, not an obstruction. He insisted that a lowering of standards would be "a fatal blow to the quality of education by the State and to the careers and happiness of great numbers of its young men and women."[7]

Unlike President Davis, however, President Sproul had great difficulty selling this idea to the legislature. As the Depression continued to cast its shadow over the sunny republic, the notion that UC's aura of elitism was in the state's best interest became harder and harder for legislators to accept. Commenting ruefully on the delicate balance he had to maintain for his university, Sproul noted, "[UC] suffers the inevitable penalty of leadership: envy, denial, and detraction. On the one hand it is criticized for being too aristocratic, on the other for being too democratic."[8]

Early in 1933, Sproul enlisted his faculty in the fight to stop regional colleges, using the tactic of calling for a consideration of the university's purpose and standards. He asked his newly formed Committee on Educational Policy "to ascertain whether the time may not have arrived for alteration in our present academic system."[9] The committee obliged by crafting a statement that defended the "present academic system" and defined the university's intellectual work sharply against the training work that would be undertaken should the regional college movement succeed:

> The service of the University is not limited to the training of experts. It must also provide for the education of men competent to analyze and weigh measures of public importance, and, in the interest of the public, to fit the recommendations of experts to existing conditions.[10]

Mindful, as well, of the university's position as the bastion of conservatism in a decade that had already seen more than one hundred strikes, deep social upheaval, and an upwelling of interest in Communism, the Committee on Educational Policy stressed the stabilizing influence that the university's graduates would offer California's turbulent society:

> The University must provide the largest possible number of individuals capable of discussing and forming judgments upon the many issues which in our democracy are submitted to the people . . . The State is dependent upon the University for men whose judgment is characterized by discrimination and balance, is free from servitude to temporary feelings and emotions . . . [11]

This statement of the university's work was presented to the Academic Senate with the comment that "educated persons are in substantial agreement regarding this, but it is often not understood by the public at large." Further, the Committee on Educational Policy's chair offered his vision of the university "as a guide for dealing with external as well as internal problems."[12]

One of the "internal problems" was finding a place for those students Sproul had to enroll in order to maintain his insistence that regional colleges were not needed. With misgivings, the Committee on Educational Policy recommended establishing an experimental curriculum (of four to five years' duration) for generalists, those whose vocation lay in "business, community life, and home-making." They did not assume this task with relish, but pressed on because "it has been urged repeatedly upon the Committee."[13]

About that same time, a number of tasks were urged on the Committee on Subject A, as well. A considerable volume of complaints about the exam and the Subject A requirement had been lodged from within, by university faculty, and from without, by high school teachers and administrators, as well as parents of high school students. Complaints about Subject A were nothing new, of course; when periods of high demand for enrollment coincide with budget crises, rhetoric about the university's standards always heats up. And by the 1930s, the Subject A requirement had served for some fifty years as one of the more public indices of UC's standards.

This time the Committee on Subject A was asked to investigate not whether too many—or too few—students were passing, but that whether the *right ones* were passing. The Subject A requirement was a point of friction in the relationship between the university and the high schools, and the university was in a particularly vulnerable position just then, because of its stand against regional colleges. It behooved the university to nurture its relationship with the high schools, and an investigation of Subject A was a reasonable place to start. A reasonably safe place, to boot, because even if the investigation exposed flaws in the in the exam design, it would show that the University of California was welcoming—without conditions—more students than ever before. In 1930–31, only 29 percent of the students who took the Subject A exam failed, the lowest failure rate since the exam was established.

Behind this odd question of whether or not the right students were passing lay the results of a study, published in 1929, investigating the relationship between the grades students earned in their high school courses and on the Subject A exam (Talbott 1929). The study found that students' performance on the Subject A exam was not even distantly correlated to their performance in their English courses, or in any other courses. Rather, a successful Subject A exam most closely correlated with a high IQ (Talbott 1929).[14]

In its report to the Academic Council, the committee readily acknowledged that "many high school students and teachers believe that passing the exam [in Subject A] is a matter of chance." The Committee on Subject A tested that claim during the 1930 scoring session by choosing at random fifty exams from the stack of approximately eight hundred exams already scored, removing the score and identifying marks, and resubmitting the exam to the original scorer for a second reading. The reliability of the scorers, concluded the committee, "cannot be regarded as satisfactory."[15]

Far more satisfactory, the committee argued, would be a different sort of exam, one less dependent upon the vagaries of scorers. That element of chance would be eliminated by the addition of a grammar and usage section to supplement the essay. The Academic Council agreed to this proposed change. From 1930 on, along with the essay, examinees would complete a supplemental objective test of grammar and usage. The 1931 form comprised eighty items: thirty-six discrete-point grammar items, a nine-item spelling section, ten sentence-structure items, a five-item punctuation subtest, a ten-item capitalization subtest, and a ten-sentence diction subtest (Johnson 1941, 323). The addition of an objective section was accompanied by a refinement in scoring procedure. If a student passed the essay and earned a high score on the grammar and usage questions, he passed into the university without conditions. If he or she passed one part of the exam and failed the other, his or her essay was subjected to a second or third reading (Duff 1945, 3).

The failure rate in 1931 rose to 34 percent (up from 29 percent in 1930). This increase suggests either that the students had not prepared for the new grammar and usage supplement, or that the new procedure of second and third readings brought students' work under closer scrutiny. A severe climate of complaint prevailed within the university, prompting the Academic Senate to appoint a Special Committee on Subject A—not the regular, standing committee—in 1931. The Special Committee found necessary "a check on the literacy of university [e]ntrants," complaining that from 1928 to 1931 some "33 percent of all entering students have not been able to pass a simple examination in the writing of their mother tongue"[16] (Johnson 1941, 333).

The following year the failure rate dropped to 28 percent. This decline to an all-time low stifled complaints from without, but did nothing to moderate the climate of complaint that prevailed within the university. In that time of high demand for admission to the university, the question still remained among the faculty as to whether the right students were being accepted into their classrooms unconditionally. More students may have passed the Subject A examination, but the *examiners* were thought to have failed. The exam's failure to catch out more students and hold them for Subject A was said to place a burden on the faculty outside of the Subject A Department. The Special Committee's plaint that "it seems unfair to expect an instructor to take time from his special subject to drill students in a technique which he ought to be able to take for granted" had wide currency. As did the committee members' query as to whether "it is just to overload the lower division work of one department [English] by turning it into a filter for the University as a whole."[17]

In 1931 Guy West, professor of English and member of the Committee on Subject A, found a significant correlation between students' Subject A exam results and their scores on the Nelson-Denny reading test. Interested, doubtless, that his department not become "a filter," he recommended that a reading and vocabulary section be added to the exam (West 1931). This was done two years later.[18]

Meanwhile, in 1933, Merton E. Hill, director of admissions at the University of California, published a report of his study that focused on the predictive value of the Subject A exam. He found that there was no significant relationship between a student's performance on the exam and on his or her success in English coursework at the university. Hill did find a positive correlation between a student's performance on the exam and on his or her success in the university's course in public speaking. Hill was surprised, having thought that Subject A exam results would have more value as a source of information to his office in the decision whether or not to admit a student.

The University of California could not, of course, use the Subject A exam as an entrance exam. Those 33 percent deemed "incapable of passing a simple exam in the writing of their mother tongue," yet at the top of their high school classes, were a most important element of President Sproul's argument that there was need for but one university. Director Hill's report disappeared without comment by the administration.

Commentary on the inadequacy of the Subject A exam continued, however, and by 1934, a Subject A exam was in place that asked students to write an essay, answer grammar questions, demonstrate their reading comprehension, and display their range of vocabulary. The failure rate hovered at 33 percent.

By 1935, the Subject A examiners were having to cope with an unexpectedly high number of split scores. That is, more students were passing the objective sections but failing the essay. Rather than revisit the proposition that grammar questions were a valid indirect measure of writing ability, the examiners elected to warn the high schools against teaching to the test. The 1935 "Bulletin of the Examination in Subject A," circulated to high school teachers, cautioned against conducting "a disproportionate amount of mechanical drills on punctuation and minor points of grammar which have relatively little to do with the problem of clear and forceful expression of ideas."[19]

In 1935, the most clear and forceful idea about who should be admitted to higher education came from the legislature: that year the state enacted legislation that enabled the development and funding of a regional college system, and Sproul had lost the battle for one university. The University of California was no longer the only mouth to be fed from state funds.

CHAPTER 5

"The Hordes . . . Invade the Campus"

It is regrettable that we permit so many students to secure a degree from this institution when their ability to use their native language is as poor as it often is.

A. R. Gordon. Committee on Educational Policy Meeting Minutes, July 18, 1946. UC Berkeley Library Archives.

BORN SO SOON AFTER California's crippling general strike and her first (but certainly not last) Red Scare, this new system of regional colleges, rechristened "state colleges" in 1935, was assigned heavy political duties. According to the State Board of Education in 1939, "The state colleges more than any other group of institutions in California, face the task of interpreting democracy to society . . . [The state colleges] are qualified to assume leadership in the development of the spirit of democracy on this West Coast of America."[1]

Meanwhile, on the University of California's patch of West Coast, students were interpreting democracy through such activities as straw polls favoring the U.S. maintenance of an isolationist position in the European war, vigorous participation in peace rallies, and the opposition to compulsory ROTC (Pettitt 1966). University of California President Sproul, in his 1940 commencement address at Berkeley's Greek Theater, undertook to change students' minds, advising "American preparedness" as the "only practical course" (Stadtman 1970, 305). Shortly after that speech, Sproul proposed that UC be named an "agency of the government," and in a subsequent meeting of the Academic Senate, he pledged "the full resources of the University in service to the President and Congress" (Pettitt 1970, 305).

Sproul had strong personal convictions about America's duty to fight Hitler. He also had a strong sense that it was the university, far more than the emerging state colleges, that was qualified to promote the spirit of democracy in California. To that end, he took his campaign against neutrality to the airwaves, making numerous radio addresses. Additionally, he closed some of UC Berkeley's laboratories to foreigners, he granted leave to several of the university's physics faculty members to undertake war research at MIT, and he placed the university's cyclotron and its products at the disposal of the federal government (Stadtman 1970, 307). In early 1941, Sproul announced in a press conference that the university was offering substantial assistance to California's aircraft industry by training aircraft engineers and aerospace technicians, in offering accelerated courses in engineering, foreign languages, and weather prediction, and in conducting medical research on such problems as shock and infection (Stadtman 1970, 307).

However, not all elements of the University of California's role in the war effort were announced—or announceable. By mid-1941, the regents had begun negotiating contracts for top secret research, and, by 1942, had committed the energies of Ernest O. Lawrence and his colleagues to conduct research on the separation of uranium-235. By mid-1943, the University of California's war contracts with the federal government, secret and publicly disclosed, amounted to just under $10 million (Douglass 2000). In 1943, as well, the Manhattan Project, guided by physics professor J. Robert Oppenheimer, brought the university substantially—and fatefully—closer to being an agency of the government, as Sproul had proposed. Overall, between 1940 and 1945, the University of California received over $57 million in war contracts with the U.S. government (Douglass 2000).

The university was certainly not alone in hurling its energies into the war. California herself received in excess of $10 billion in war production grants during that period (Beck and Williams 1972). World War II was profoundly transformative of California's economy, wrenching her out of the Great Depression. Between 1939 and 1944, California agriculture rebounded, and then some, with total production increasing 300 percent (Douglass 2000). In 1944, California's agricultural output reached well over $1.5 billion (Douglass 2000). Many agricultural workers had migrated to the war-fueled manufacturing sector, and many, of course, to the theaters of war. The resultant labor shortage improved what had been grim working conditions in the fields, packing sheds, and canneries. The shortage of workers also accelerated the mechanization of planting and harvesting processes.

Because of the war, California's manufacturing was similarly sprung from the torpors of the Depression. As early as 1938, Lockheed was flush with orders from abroad, filling an order for Japan for planes designated "commercial aircraft," and beginning manufacture of two hundred warplanes for Britain. These planes, later known as Hudson Bombers, would come to contribute mightily to Britain's air defense, and would occupy a large segment of Lockheed's production manifest. Before the war ended, Lockheed had built three thousand Hudsons for Britain. By 1945, Lockheed employed ninety-four thousand workers, and Douglas had built in excess of $1 billion worth of planes (Douglass 2000).

Shipbuilding and steel production further strengthened California's economy in the war years. Kaiser Shipyards employed 100,000 workers at the San Francisco Bay Area's Richmond Yards alone. By V-J Day, they had built 727 ships for the U.S. government, and had been a principal manufacturer of those vessels so critical to the war effort, the Liberty Ships. As early as 1940, Kaiser Shipbuilding had landed a U.S. government contract to build 30 cargo ships for Britain, this order a part of Roosevelt's Lend-Lease Program (Johnson 1993). War production boomed in related industries as well, bringing the San Francisco Bay Area alone over $7 million in government contracts for the refining of oil, the generation of electricity, and the processing of food (Johnson 1993).

The Bay Area's economy boomed most ferociously because of the war, but it was by no means the only region of California to prosper. San Diego attracted intense military and war-industry development, its population growing by 110 percent between 1940 and 1947. The population of Los Angeles and Long Beach increased substantially as well (Johnson 1993). By the end of hostilities, California's ailing economy had been transfused with $35 billion in government contracts. Her population grew more than any other state's during that period, with in-migration totaling over 1.5 million; 33 percent of these people settled in the Bay Area (Johnson 1993).

The nation looked at California in a very different way after the war, and, indeed, California looked at herself differently. Her enormous advances in industrialization, both in manufacturing and agriculture, accrued to her both prestige and wealth. (California's liquid assets in 1945 amounted to $15 billion [Beck and Williams 1972].) Significantly for the story of her industry in higher education, Californians learned, perhaps before many of their fellow Americans did, the importance of a highly educated, skilled technical workforce.

It was the confluence of these postwar circumstances—California's wealth, prestige, industrialization, and appreciation of a highly educated workforce—that led her "one university" to begin its transformation. The University of California of the 1930s was a public institution struggling to hold on to the lion's share of the diminishing higher-education dollar and the taxpayer's waning favor. The University of California that emerged from the war was a research facility of value to the entire nation, and not only California. This university was, however, just beginning to glimpse its future; it would be several decades, and more than a few political firestorms, before it grew into a full realization of its national role as a research university.

In the years immediately following the war, what UC *did* realize was the power of the federal government to confer grace upon higher education. The GI Bill of 1945 was a new sort of government contract that brought a huge influx of federal money to higher education.[2] And a huge influx of a new kind of student, not necessarily either well heeled or well spoken. The University of California, like every other American university and college, was eager to accept the federal monies that these veterans' enrollment represented. California, like every other state, was grateful for the sacrifices these veterans had made, and her university was willing to sacrifice some of its admission standards to increase the number of veterans it could admit.

In point of fact, the University of California had embarked upon a relaxation of admission standards a few years before the GI Bill was passed. During 1943, 1944, and 1945, enrollment had dropped precipitously as men went to war and women took war-industry work (Johnson 1993). The

Berkeley campus was by no means deserted, however; it housed training facilities for various military specialists. The university's Morrison Library Committee reported to the Academic Senate with pride that "with or without a University connection, a large number of the 950 readers who use the library each week were men in uniform."[3] As welcome as these men in uniform were, they weren't filling the class rosters.

The drop in enrollment was such that in January of 1943, the newly formed Emergency Executive Committee recommended that the University of California relax its standards for admission for the 1943–44 academic year, to enroll students who had not graduated from high school, but who had completed two and a half years of senior high and maintained a B average.[4] The members of the Emergency Executive Committee were guided by compassion as well as the need to raise enrollments. In proposing the admission of students whose high school educations had been interrupted by the war, they addressed the need to recognize that "many young men had been rapidly matured by their service."[5]

In 1943 through 1945, higher education benefited, as well, from the compassion of newly elected Governor Earl Warren. He was eager to expand higher-education opportunities for Californians, particularly veterans. Warren had inherited a whopping $90 million wartime surplus in general funds, and the expectation of a $230 million surplus by 1945 (Douglass 2000). He was also about to inherit some seven hundred thousand veterans looking for jobs, and some six hundred thousand unemployed former war-industry workers. Not surprisingly, his interest in developing higher-education opportunities extended beyond liberal arts schooling to embrace professional and technical training. For this he was eager both to fund UC-based research programs aimed at developing new industries, and to fund the establishment of new state colleges and junior colleges.

The first funding prospect, research monies for UC, delighted Sproul, Earl Warren's old classmate at Berkeley, but the second prospect, the expansion of the state colleges, gave him pause. When they were boys together in the Cal Band, Clarinetist Warren may have taken his marching orders from Drum Major Sproul, but now it was Governor Warren who called the tune.

In his attempts to plan for expanded higher-education opportunities in California, Warren was in close step with the federal government. In 1944, Roosevelt's Educational Policies Commission recommended the expansion of junior colleges and state colleges in order to provide "an education appropriate to free men in American democracy" (National Policies Commission 1944, 246). Similarly, the National Resources Planning Board advocated the development of higher education throughout the U.S., both to promote socioeconomic mobility, and to prevent the rise of Communism. A Communist movement, it was inferred, would occur if a postwar recession and its attendant unemployment brought about widespread labor strife.

This fear of Communist-inspired labor unrest was particularly strong in California, given her strike-scarred Depression years. Governor Warren's plan to find a place for "anyone who would benefit from higher education" (Douglass 2000, 174) had the merit of up-skilling California's workforce. Importantly, it also would serve to divert into higher education thousands of veterans and displaced war-industry workers who would otherwise be queuing immediately for places in California's inevitably shaky postwar labor market.[6]

Thus, the expansion of higher education in California came to be predicated on the expectation that her campuses would help save California from Communist infiltration. The citizenry, the legislature, and many of the regents subscribed to this theory of the aims of education. This assumption, that the University of California would serve the state as a bulwark against Communism, was to come under question most stridently in the 1950s and 1960s, with very powerful repercussions for the Berkeley campus in particular. However, in the period immediately following the war, the University of California had few questions about the nature of its role in the defense of the democratic way of life in America. Rather, the university was engaged in a more local question: how to embrace democratic values in its admissions policy while continuing to grow into its new role as a prestigious research university. In 1945, Sproul indicated the University of California's reluctance to enter into this embrace in an address to the regents, asking "Shall we be prepared for the hordes . . . invad[ing] the campus?" (Pettit 1966, 77).

The Board of Admissions responded with a proposal to change university policy so that the board had the right to exercise a "reasonably liberal interpretation" of admissions requirements so that "applicants with minor deficiencies" could be enrolled as regular students. Applicants with "graver deficiencies" were to be considered as well, but for admission to "special student status."[7] The Board listed the following criteria for GI-Bill-era admission decisions: "school records, war service records, letters of recommendation, results of Subject A test and other aptitude tests as may seem appropriate, findings based on conferences with applicants."[8]

In 1945, then, the university, or its Board of Admissions, set itself the difficult balancing task of "maintaining as far as possible the spirit of the [prewar] standards of admission while assuring to each veteran who applies for admission the maximum of opportunity and success."[9] There were quite a lot of Californians, veterans and otherwise, who were expecting the opportunity for success, however, and President Sproul was decidedly thrown off balance by the huge demand on the resources of his "one university."

The administration's bumpy balancing act soon drew critical reviews from the faculty. In 1946 the Emergency Executive Committee met to discuss the "inadequacy of training in oral and written English among so many successful candidates for Bachelor's degrees."[10] A letter from a member of that committee detailing students' "deplorable deficiencies in the use of English" was read into the minutes of the Academic Senate.[11] This letter noted collateral deficiencies in the Subject A examination, which failed to "screen out" those deficient students, and in Subject A instruction, which failed to correct their deficiency.

In immediate response, the Committee on Educational Policy at the University of California, Berkeley convened a special meeting on "Students' English." The committee's diagnosis of the malady was that students write badly because they think badly: "Students lack clearness and precision in thought, so they express themselves without either clearness or precision."[12] Furthermore, to complete the circuit, students think badly because they haven't learned to write better: "[Students have lacked] the opportunity and incentive for the attainment of a high standard of English expression."[13] Evidently, for these GIs turned Golden Bears, war had not only been hell; it had been a disincentive for attaining a high standard of English expression.

Throughout 1946, the legislature was restive, growing less convinced by the day of the university's ability to meet the needs of California's citizens. Sproul had already been maneuvered by a shrewd legislator into accepting the college at Santa Barbara as a campus of the University of

California in 1943, and feared that further shotgun weddings with state colleges would dilute the university's budget even further. Sproul held firm to his plan to deny UC Santa Barbara a research function or a role in graduate education. He managed to put the best possible face on the legislated acquisition of Santa Barbara, however, proclaiming that campus's importance as an undergraduate institution and provider of a liberal education, a "Williams of the West" (Douglass 2000, 169). This spin was about more than hoarding all the prestige for Berkeley and UCLA, however.[14] It was about preserving UC's constitutional status as a public trust, and about preventing legislative incursions.

Again, Sproul was fighting a losing battle against the expansion of the number of higher education institutions. Additional legislative unrest that year was reflected in the swarm of bills to convert junior colleges into four-year state colleges. In 1946 alone, legislation was proposed to convert into state college status the following: Stanislaus Junior College, Mt. Shasta Junior College, Stanislaus Polytechnic Institute, Fresno School of Agriculture, San Luis Obispo Polytechnic School, and Pomona Polytechnic School. Sproul bemoaned all of this, calling it "dangerous expansion" (Douglass 2000, 128).

Most worrisome of all to Sproul were bills to expand certain existing state colleges into institutions with a research function and the capacity to grant graduate degrees. As Sproul saw it, the University of California simply could not afford this loss of its unique status. Sproul executed a range of defensive maneuvers in order to assert the university's prestige and special status. Important to my story about the rhetoric of remediation is his call to the Academic Senate to address the problem of student writing.[15] As before, a burst of rhetoric about the failure of many applicants and students to live up to the university's exacting standards had the effect of reminding everyone just how high the university's standards were.

The failure rate on the Subject A exam averaged 40 percent in those immediate postwar years, in spite of the examiners' inclusion of topics they had thought would be congenial to veterans. For example, the following topic was an option on several of the Subject A exams administered between 1946 and 1951:

> Discuss reasons both for and against having professional military men in
> high political office.[16]

Examples of students' work on this topic were unavailable in the Subject A Archives, as was information about the popularity of this option among the examinees, but it is not hard to imagine that this was a frequently chosen topic during Douglas MacArthur's failed bid for the presidency on the Christian-National Party ticket, and Eisenhower's first campaign, in 1950–51.

Similarly, the topic

> Discuss the ways of improving your means of transportation if you owned a thirteen-year-old car and had only $300 to spend. (Subject A Archives)

yielded disappointing results, even though California must surely have led the world in automobiles per capita by this time. The quality of students' writing continued to be a thorn in the university's side throughout the postwar years of expanded demand for access to higher education. In 1949, President Sproul called for a review of the quality of writing produced by all University of California undergraduates, from newly admitted freshmen to seniors, noting "widespread dissatisfaction among employers, instructors, and students themselves."[17]

It might have been a bit disingenuous for Sproul to have suggested that the widespread dissatisfaction was focused solely, or even primarily, upon students' writing skills. Dissatisfaction with the University of California— its students, faculty, and indeed its president—had spread far beyond undergraduate grammar and usage at this delicate moment in California's life. California had embraced the postwar anti-Communist movement with her usual enthusiasm for crusades. After his defeat as General MacArthur's running mate, California State Senator John Tenney returned to Sacramento and levied substantial damages on the reputation of the University of California that reverberated throughout the nation. Tenney's Joint Fact-Finding Committee on Un-American Activities, established in 1942, but largely dormant during the war years, began in 1945 to urge a vigorous and highly publicized war on the University of California. Throughout the second half of the decade, Tenney's committee subpoenaed witness after witness in a campaign to expose the University of California as a sanctuary for Communist educators, if not an outright rookery for young collegiate converts to Communism (Kerr 2002).

Particularly galling for the Joint Fact-Finding Committee was the participation of University of California students in strikes within the movie industry throughout 1945 and 1946 (Johnson 1993). Unemployment was low in booming postwar Southern California, and the unions had muscle to flex, making demands of the captains of that most iconic of Californian industries, the film studios. Strikers, including UCLA students, were met with a heavy police response, tear gas, and accusations of Communist insurgency. The students' visible support of this strike fed Senator Tenney's darkest suspicion, that the University of California had been infiltrated by Communist and Communist-sympathetic faculty who were professing the faith to the sunny republic's best and brightest young people. He struck hard and fast.

In January of 1949, Senator Tenney introduced a bill to revoke the constitutional amendment of 1868 that had established UC's status as a public trust, and that had laid the university's governance squarely in the hands of the regents (Kerr 2002). This constitutional amendment, called the Organic Act, had for some eighty years assured the University of California freedom from legislative tinkering with the budget at the line-item level, and had provided autonomy in academic appointments and departmental matters. Beyond abolishing that autonomy, Tenney's legislation proposed to require a loyalty oath of all university faculty and staff.[18] During World War II, the practice had been established of requiring anyone hired at the University of California to pledge to support and defend the constitutions of the United States and California. Indeed, the practice continues in 2009. However, Tenney's legislation of 1949 proposed to expand the pledge to include the assertion,

> I do not believe in nor am a member of, nor do I support any party or organization that advocates, believes in, or teaches overthrow of the U.S. government, by force or illegal or unconstitutional means. (Starr 2002, 282)

Tenney's bill was thought to have had a good chance for success; Communism's threat to the American way of life was very real in the minds of California's taxpayers (Starr 2002). By the time the Joint Fact-Finding Committee on Un-American Activities ran out of steam, or witnesses, it had interrogated hundreds of Californians, casting shadows on the reputations and careers of University of California faculty members, high school teachers, union members, Hollywood figures, and many others. Making good his 1946 boast that "UC is no sacred cow" (Starr 2002, 312), the committee even interrogated Doris Heller, wife of Regent Walter Heller, and later a regent herself. Despite all this effort and all these interrogations, the fact-finding committee failed to find facts enough to support even one indictment.

At this time, of course, another concerned Californian was making even more strenuous—and far more public—efforts to fight Communism. His arena, however, was national. Richard Nixon made his way to the U.S. House of Representatives largely by casting his liberal Democrat opponent, Jerry Voorhis, as soft on Communism. Representative Nixon quickly was appointed to the House Un-American Activities Committee.

The House Un-American Activities Committee was the immensely more powerful big brother to Tenney's California committee, and when it set its sights on Southern California, particularly Hollywood, the repercussions were even more spectacular. The story of the House Un-American Activities Committee's systemic abuse of its investigatorial ambit, as well as its depredations of the careers and lives of the people it targeted, is a tale that has been widely told. It stands, at best, as a cautionary tale about the potential dangers of congressional overreach, and at worst, as a shameful abandonment of democratic values.

In 1946, however, the House Un-American Activities Committee's allegations must have seemed to many Americans terrifying evidence of the threat within our borders. These allegations must have been especially shocking for Californians who, the committee insisted, had been nurturing a very Red, very influential subculture in her southern reaches.

Three years later, the committee shifted its lens to Northern California and commenced hearings on alleged wartime subversion at Berkeley's Radiation Laboratory, and on alleged Communist infiltration of the Manhattan Project. J. Robert Oppenheimer's political indiscretions, Communist sympathies and associations, as well as alleged deeper involvement with the Communist Party, had kept the Bay Area field office of the FBI well occupied from 1942 on, when he began sketching out preliminary concepts of an atomic weapon in his campus office next to Berkeley's Campanile (Starr 2002).

By 1949, then, the University of California was feeling the destabilizing effects of the crusade against Communism. Two powerful currents—Senator Tenney's proposed legislation to bring the Red University under direct, intense legislative control by revoking its status as a public trust and compelling its faculty and staff to sign a loyalty oath; and the House Un-American Activities Committee's investigations of alleged Communist infiltration of Berkeley's wartime atomic research—were about to collide, and threatened to pull the University of California into a treacherous undertow. In spring of 1949, President Sproul proposed to the regents that the university draw up its own loyalty oath, both to head off the legislature and to offset any damages that the committee might wreak on its reputation. The regents quickly assented. All University of California faculty were advised that, if they wished to be reappointed for the 1949–50 academic year, they would have to sign a loyalty oath. In those days, faculty were given annual contracts. The University of California was unique among the major universities in not providing continuous tenure to its faculty (Kerr 2002).

Faculty opposition arose immediately, especially at Los Angeles and Berkeley. Prominent among the anti-loyalty-oath faculty at Berkeley were Provost (and former Vice President) Monroe Deutsch and Professor of Economics Clark Kerr. Ernest Kantorowicz, professor of history, likened the loyalty oath requirement to Mussolini's demands for loyalty in 1931 and Hitler's in 1933 (Starr 2002). Faculty saw the loyalty oath as violative of academic freedom, and a gnawing reminder that the University of California did not offer its professoriate continuous tenure.

President Sproul was generally taken aback by faculty resistance to what seemed a pragmatic and politic maneuver to keep UC autonomous of the legislature and congenial to the taxpayers. Gambling that faculty resistance and rhetoric would play itself out, Sproul extended the deadline for signing the oath. What Sproul saw as a pragmatic move, many regents saw as a conciliatory move. They met it with outrage. Several regents' support of the oath stemmed more, perhaps, from ideology than pragmatism. Regent Giannini, in the April 22, 1950 edition of the *San Francisco Chronicle*, was particularly forthright in professing his anti-Communism and his support of the loyalty oath: "I want to organize twentieth century vigilantes," he insisted, "who will unearth communists and communism in all its sordid aspects" (Stewart 1950, 94). The Hearst-owned press joined the fray, castigating the anti-loyalty-oath professors sharply and regularly throughout the years the controversy raged.[19]

The loyalty oath controversy brought the university notoriety beyond California. On October 21, 1950, in "The Record of Communism at UCLA," the *Saturday Evening Post* described how a small minority of fellow travelers at UCLA were endangering the entire university (Starr 2002, 325). That same year *Life Magazine* covered UC Berkeley's dismissal of much-lauded —and clearly non-Communist—sixty-four-year-old Professor of Psychology Edward Tolman for his refusal to sign the oath: "At the University of California last week a very sad fact was being proved . . . [I]n opposing communism, Americans sometimes create another evil" (1950, 431).

Nationwide, the academic community clearly saw this evil. Incensed by the action taken by the University of California, faculty assemblies of great universities across the country drafted memoranda of support for their California colleagues who refused to sign the loyalty oath. Assemblies at Columbia, Harvard, Michigan, Princeton, Wisconsin, and Yale prepared such documents, and faculty at the University of Chicago went so far as to raise a fund to help dismissed University of California faculty members meet their expenses (Starr 2002).

The University of California was besieged from all sides. Its hard-won prestige among universities had plummeted, and California's citizenry found little to admire about their university. Expressions of outrage at the "Red University" had helped to propel Nixon into the U.S. Senate. Anti-Communist sentiment among Californians was crystallized when the U.S. commenced a police action in Korea in June of 1950, and swiftly mobilized the California National Guard's Fortieth Infantry Division (Starr 2002).

While the California National Guard was working its way through Korea, the lawsuit against the university's loyalty oath was working its way through the courts. In 1951, the California Supreme Court ruled that the dismissals of the non-signers at UCLA and UC Berkeley were unconstitutional. This ruling restored those faculty members to their positions,[20] but it did nothing to recoup Sproul's losses. He was hopelessly compromised by the loyalty oath controversy. In 1951, the regents voted on a reorganization of governance, with chancellors appointed at each campus, and the president's responsibilities substantively diminished. This reorganization of the University of California abolished what Clark Kerr later referred to as a "centralized system with a single source of decision-making like Napoleonic France" (Kerr 2002, 220).

Sproul stayed on as the University of California's president through 1958, but with greatly diminished stature. In this new, decentralized system, it fell to UC Berkeley's chancellor to right the foundering flagship. And at least some of the ballast was to be provided by the rhetoric of remediation.

CHAPTER 6

"The Decencies of English"

Dissatisfaction over undergraduates' incorrect and incompetent use of English in their written exercises is both widespread and perennial. The facts are not in doubt, nor can we doubt the sincerity of those of the University faculty who express their concern at the situation. The problem is to assign responsibility . . .

Committee on Educational Policy Report, November 1955. UC Berkeley Library Archives.

CLARK KERR WAS the somewhat unlikely appointee for chancellor at Berkeley. Indeed, Sproul did not appoint Kerr as soon as chancellorships were created; he retained his close control over Berkeley for another year. Kerr, as an early and vocal opponent of the loyalty oath, but one who eventually signed, was acceptable—albeit reservedly—to both faculty and regents. Arch-conservative Regents Ahlport and Neylan abstained from voting on Kerr's appointment, and Regent Dickson made his sentiments known shortly after Kerr took office by grabbing Kerr's lapels after a meeting and addressing him as the "Red Chancellor" (Kerr 2002, 131).

Chancellor Kerr immediately set about restoring the University of California's reputation among the great universities, and among California's taxpayers. He saw very clearly his responsibility to pull UC Berkeley back from the brink to which the loyalty oath controversy had brought it. He sought to upgrade the quality of Berkeley's faculty and its departments. In the first few years of his chancellorship, Kerr worked closely with his old ally and friend, A. R. Davis,[1] dean of the College of Letters and Science, to clear out the deadwood, denying reappointment to "a lot of postwar GI-rush hires" whom Kerr found "possibly adequate, but certainly not distinguished scholars" (Kerr 2002, 62).

Dean Davis had been working to rehabilitate the university's reputation among California's other institutions of higher education even before Kerr was inaugurated. In 1951, Davis was a vocal participant in several of a swarm of university committee meetings convened to discuss the problem —some participants called it a crisis—caused by the perceived deficiencies of the transfer students that the university accepted from the state's junior colleges. The university was, of course, obliged to accept junior college transfers who presented the required credits; the university needed to keep the junior colleges' support in Sacramento in battles against expansion of the four-year state colleges. But the university was not obliged to accept these junior college transfers without making a point of their deficiencies. The university couldn't clear out the GI-rush *student* deadwood, as Kerr and Davis were doing with the faculty, but it could distance itself from these students. The meetings spawned by President Sproul's complaint about widespread dissatisfaction were prime venues for distinguishing the University of California's high standards from those of lesser institutions.

"Whether the requirements of the [Subject A] test be surmounted during high school or on the rack of a sub-freshman course," opined one Professor Sherwood Bronson, "it is generally assumed that such a grade confers upon the student . . . a state of grace in which thenceforth he may rest untroubled and secure. But this assumption, shared by students and faculty alike, may be over-sanguine."[2] The "Subject A problem," or at least the GI-rush version of it, became the topic of numerous meetings in the early 1950s, engaging the attentions of the Committee on Educational Policy, the Subject A Committee, the Liaison Committee on the Subject A Problem, the offices of Admissions and Relations with Schools, and others.

In March of 1951, the Committee on Educational Policy recommended that every transfer student be required to take the Subject A examination, even if he'd passed a purportedly equivalent composition course at his junior college.[3] (Most of the transfers were male in 1951. Many veterans were still making their way through higher education on the GI Bill.) This recommendation was promptly seconded by the Committee on Subject A.[4]

Just as promptly, the Board of Admissions and Relations with Schools saw the profound political problems inherent in this joint recommendation. They arranged for the creation of a Liaison Committee on the Subject A Problem, which was to "make a comprehensive study of the Subject A problem."[5]

The membership of the Liaison Committee was drawn from University of California faculty, junior college faculty, state college faculty, representatives of the offices of Admissions and Relations with Schools, and representatives from the Subject A Office. At the meeting, an all-day marathon on the Berkeley campus, Professor S. R. Jaynes, chair of the Subject A Committee, and Professor Evans, of English, very substantially upped the ante. They proposed that the Subject A Committee and the Subject A Office be given jurisdiction over *all* undergraduate students, and be allowed to administer an examination of writing proficiency not only to junior college transfers, but also to students who had entered as freshmen with College Entrance Examination Board scores that had heretofore exempted them from the Subject A requirement. The aggrieved tones in which Jaynes couched his proposal suggested that he and his Subject A committee had long borne the brunt of complaints about the quality of students' writing: "The committee feels that it cannot discharge its responsibilities unless all of the University's students come under its authority."[6] However, Director of Admissions Hiram Spindt had in mind other of the university's responsibilities—political ones. He warned the committee that such a move would "set back the University's relations with the junior colleges twenty years."[7]

Professor Evans responded with a complaint about the relations of the Office of Admissions with the Subject A Committee. He pointed out that Office of Admissions frequently pressed the Subject A Committee to make hasty decisions on the equivalence of composition courses offered at various junior colleges. In their interest in maintaining smooth relations with the junior colleges, he noted, Admissions often failed to provide the Subject A Committee with information about the content or quality of these courses. Evans asked for broader discretion for the Subject A Committee to decline to accept junior college courses.

Evans argued that, if the members of this specially assembled Liaison Committee on the Subject A problem really wanted to do something to remedy the widespread dissatisfaction about which President Sproul had complained, they would support the expansion of the Subject A Office's portfolio and permit it to mandate instruction, if appropriate, for junior students, transfers, and others, beyond the Subject A level, despite the costliness of such a solution. "There is indeed a crisis," insisted Evans, "and immediate and decisive action should be taken by the University."[8]

Immediate and decisive action is precisely what Dean Davis and Director Spindt did not want to happen. Davis framed his objections to Jaynes's and Evans's proposals jurisprudentially: it was the Academic Senate that had the right to make decisions about transfer requirements, not the Subject A Committee. Director Spindt held to his forceful objection, repeating that such an arrogation by the Subject A Committee "would be regarded as a severe criticism of the junior colleges of the State."[9]

The Office of Relations with Schools saw the political consequences of an expanded role for the Subject A Office as well. Associate Director Grace Bird expressed her office's "astonishment and distress" at the proposal of testing junior transfer students and of mandating upper-division writing instruction. She agreed that such an exam would chill the University of California's amicable, and politically very important, relationship with the junior colleges. At the very least, she insisted, the proposal is fraught with procedural errors, in that consultation had not been sought from the Junior College Conference Committee, the High School Affiliates Committee, the Committee on Coordination with State Colleges, and the California Committee for the Study of Education.[10]

The Subject A Committee proffered the information that several prestigious institutions administered junior-level writing examinations and offered instruction past the freshman year. This cut no ice with the Office of Relations with Schools, however: "Harvard, Yale, Michigan, and Wisconsin's [testing practices] are not applicable to the California situation.[11] No elaboration was offered as to how these other institutions did not present the same situation as California's "one university" did, but it is not too difficult to figure out. California had, by then, far more junior colleges than any other state. Each of them had students eager to transfer into four-year colleges. Some of these institutions had ambitions to expand into four-year colleges themselves. California also had a slew of state colleges in competition with the university. Each state college was eager to develop its prestige, enrollments, instructional offerings, state appropriations, and its share of GI-Bill monies. Some were eager to develop research and graduate programs.

Representatives of the Subject A Committee had failed to recognize—or, more likely, had chosen to challenge—the rhetorical moment: this discussion about underperforming junior colleges and low-attaining GIs was not so much a quest for a solution to the problem of poor student writing as it was a means through which the University of California might assert its high standards.

Finally, California's "situation" included a delicate alliance between the university and the junior colleges against the interests of the state colleges. There were many reasons to steer clear of a testing program in writing proficiency for the University of California's juniors. It's just that none of those reasons had anything to do with students' writing proficiency. The "comprehensive study of the Subject A problem" that occupied so much time in 1951 was, well, uncomprehensive. Nothing changed, for all the discussions, except that the university was able to profess as an article of faith that veterans had to be taken in, even if they weren't quite what the University of California was used to. Gratitude demanded it. Patriotism demanded it. For California's sake, her one university would embrace the veterans, however reluctantly. And, after all, the veterans would soon be gone. All the university had to do in the meantime was lie back, and think of California.

By the following year, California's legislature had begun to articulate its reluctance to foot the bill for what it suspected were redundant services offered in the state's three segments of higher education. Early in the 1953 legislative session, the Assembly Ways and Means Committee asked what the differences were among the university, the state colleges, and the junior colleges in the training of California's young people. Ways and Means asked *how* graduates from the university were different from graduates of state colleges. They wanted to know why California's taxpayers had to pay for three institutions' version of "thirteenth" and "fourteenth" grades. They wanted to know why all this higher education wasn't yielding California the engineers and skilled technical workers that it so desperately needed. The legislature commissioned a detailed cost analysis of each segment of higher education (Douglass 2000).

This plaint about the wasteful redundancy of academic services may seem no more than an echo of Sproul's good fight for the one university, but this time the prize was something else entirely. Legislators wanted state colleges in their own districts, or they wanted programs in their state colleges that directly stimulated economic growth in their districts. And if it took some Golden Bear-baiting in Sacramento, so be it.

More than a few of the university's friends in high places had moved on. In 1953, Governor Warren was appointed chief justice of the Supreme Court.[12] He was succeeded by very conservative Lieutenant Governor Goodwin Knight. Knight's accession to office coincided with a nationwide recession, and his administration quickly called for retrenchment, if not actual retraction, of California's largesse in funding higher education. Both the Senate and the Assembly were Republican controlled, and neither house was particularly eager to accommodate the interests of California's "Red University" (Douglass 2000). The loyalty oath controversy had beaten the stuffing out of the Bear.

It was in this atmosphere of siege that the University of California became particularly sensitive to public criticism of its students' writing. The Committee on Educational Policy authorized a Prose Improvement Project, led by English professors Josephine Miles and Benjamin Lehman, to work with faculty in numerous departments to raise the quality of students' writing. This was a remarkably forward-thinking endeavor, anticipating by nearly two decades the writing-in-the-disciplines movement in higher education. Sadly, the project lasted only a few years. Led first by Miles in 1951, and soon thereafter by Lehman, the Prose Improvement Committee held the belief that a "proper final solution to the problem of teaching satisfactory prose presentation should . . . be worked out by interested departments. They and they only can make prose improvement in the University at large a well-founded, continuous, growing effort."[13]

Professor Miles collected samples of student writing from a range of departments and, in consultation with members of those departments, identified features that diminished the writers' effectiveness. Significantly, this was not simply an exercise in assessing grammar and usage errors, although, of course, those were found and noted. Miles and her consultants identified important discipline-specific omissions, such as the failure to articulate the relationship between events or principles presented in the course, inadequate or inaccurate use of the lexicon of the discipline, and failure to apply the analytical modes taught in the course.[14]

Next, the Prose Improvement Project recruited twenty graduate students from the English Department and trained them to work with students' writing. Each of these teaching assistants was then assigned to a specific course in one of the nine departments that participated in the project.[15] The TA worked with the professor of the course on developing examination questions, and on anticipating the types of writing—and displays of subject knowledge—they would produce. The TAs also worked with the students on principles of organizing and presenting the subject matter of the course, usage of the lexicon of the discipline, and grammar. The participating professors' teaching loads were reduced so that they would have time to engage in conversation with the TAs assigned to them about the expectations for students writing in their disciplines, and about ways that guidance in writing techniques could become part of the instruction of the course. Beyond consulting with the professor in charge of the course, each TA worked with the students, in lectures or smaller groups. Lehman insisted that "it is the TAs who are the immediate educators . . . the upholders of standards, the interpreters, the channelers of communication and evaluation." Some 740 undergraduates were involved in the project in 1952–53, the peak year. Some 50–75 percent of these students improved by one grade between the midterm and the final. Improvement was noted both in understanding of the subject matter and language use.[16]

The Prose Improvement Committee's project continued for a few years in the early 1950s, but it did not thrive. This was, in part, because the participating departments did not offer as much support as this ambitious project required. Both Lehman and Miles had stressed the importance of each participating department's appointing a "vice chairman in charge of TAs and readers, a man of special aptitudes with genuine interest in the problem [of student writing]," whose job it would be to "gain the interested cooperation of his fellow department members."[17] This did not happen; departments, however concerned they might have been to improve students' prose, were either unable to find release time for professors, or were unable to find those men of special aptitudes with sufficient genuine interest in the problem.

It is important to note that the Prose Improvement Project died not just because of insufficient engagement by the departments. The English Department found itself unable to appoint a sufficient number of TAs to the project. In this time of booming undergraduate enrollment, the English Department had difficulty enough appointing graduate students to TA the English Department's own courses. There simply weren't enough to go around. Additionally, Lehman noted an ethical problem in recruiting more graduate students: "It would be impossible to 'place' a doubled or tripled number of those who [would take] the doctorate."[18]

Finally, it must be considered that the Prose Improvement Project suffered for lack of support from the chancellor. In a letter to Roy Jastrow, chair of the Committee on Educational Policy, Professor Lehman expressed his disappointment that he had heard nothing from Chancellor Kerr regarding the Prose Improvement Committee's fate.[19]

In the fall of the 1953–54 academic year, Professor Robert Connick, representing the English Department and the Committee on Educational Policy, wrote to Chancellor Kerr, requesting funding for another year of the project, as well as monies to prepare a student handbook on writing exams and reports. This year's request was different in that it asked that the Prose Improvement Project be funded separately from the English Department. Before, the English Department and participating departments had carved, from their own budgets, the costs entailed in the Prose Improvement Project. Now, Professor Connick asked that Kerr consider the improvement of students' writing to be the work of the whole of the Berkeley campus, not just an experiment between the English Department and some interested professors from other disciplines. The funding was not forthcoming. The Prose Improvement Project persisted for a few years after that, patching together funding from various sources, but it never had the role in the university that it deserved.

The short life of the Prose Improvement Project deserves a fuller account than is offered here. The full story would stand as a tribute to the pioneering work in writing-in-the-disciplines pedagogy undertaken by Josephine Miles and Benjamin Lehman. It would stand also as an exegesis on the daunting institutional difficulties inherent in attempting such a collaborative pedagogy in a large public university.

This brief account of the Prose Improvement Project—or more particularly, its very brevity—has something to offer my story about the rhetoric of remediation. The project's failure stands for the proposition that the tradition of complaint about students' writing problems is far more robust than is the tradition of supporting pedagogies to address these problems. Admittedly, this is a trivial point; it is always easier—and thus more common—to complain about something than to fix it. Beyond this commonplace, however, lies the notion that the complaint has a life of its own, a purpose separate from the problem.

It was doubtless the case that some ill-prepared students made their way to—and through—the University of California, Berkeley, in the 1950s. It is doubtless true today. Through the years, various programs have been mounted to help these students, with various degrees of institutional longevity. Subject A is, of course, the doyenne of all of the University of California's programs to identify and address students' shortcomings. The Subject A requirement was set up when the university was in its infancy. Subject A instruction started back in the days when President Wheeler still galloped around campus on a big white horse. Yet despite the number of years Subject A has been at the university, it has never managed to get tenure. Every few years, Subject A, and more importantly, the students associated with it, are the focus of complaint and charges of inadequacy.

In the spring of 1954, President Sproul unveiled a panoply of complaints about what he perceived to be a "more fundamental weakness" in University of California students: their poor reading skills.[20] Sproul alluded to letters from concerned parents and employers, as well as expressions of outrage in the press. Drawing on a complaint from an alumnus about his two sons, both Berkeley students, Sproul maintained that students' reading problems were even graver than their writing problems and that their reading skills were well below the standards of an institution of the University of California's caliber. He tasked the Subject A Committee and the Committee on Educational Policy to conduct an investigation of the poor reading skills of students held for the Subject A requirement. He asked the Subject A Committee to look into this complaint, and to consider the usefulness of the Subject A exam for screening out poor readers. Finally, he called on the committee to propose improvements. A new rhetoric of remediation was to occupy the energies of these committees through the end of 1956, and a new series of studies on the substandardness of the students who were attempting to lumber through this proud university were to emerge.

The results of the investigation undertaken by the Subject A Committee and the Committee on Educational Policy were submitted to President Sproul and Chancellor Kerr in 1956. The committees were able to write a reassuring letter indicating that, although the Subject A study did indeed find that some 15 percent of University of California admittees were "handicapped by subnormal reading speed and comprehension,"[21] UC was in good company: the same percentage was similarly handicapped at the University of Minnesota.[22]

The Committee on Educational Policy conceded that, as an experiment, the Subject A examination might well be supplemented with a test on reading speed and comprehension, in order to more fully gauge the seriousness of the problem. Importantly, the Committee on Educational Policy reminded Sproul and Kerr that, whatever the findings from this supplemental exam, reading instruction was not the university's responsibility. The exam would merely apprise students of their shortcomings—and remind everybody else of the university's standards. Sproul agreed; he had earlier insisted that such students would have to make their own reparations, perhaps through UC Extension. The cost of this instruction, maintained Sproul, "like the cost of fitting a pair of glasses, should be borne by the student."[23]

My story of the rhetoric of remediation in the midfifties holds firm to the central theme that the remedial student has long borne a considerable load for the university. Complaining that the university's standards have been breached is a way of reminding all concerned just how high those standards are. And this assertion of superiority was certainly necessary in 1955, when the legislature considered proposals for sites for thirteen new state college campuses, and reviewed plans for enlarging the size and mission of several existing ones (Douglass 2000, 210). The 1956 legislative session put perhaps more pressure on UC to show its superiority. That year, the legislature began asking even more pointed questions about the relative costs of thirteenth and fourteenth grades at the three institutional levels (Douglass 2000, 225).

There was also legislative interest that year in converting some junior colleges into four-year state colleges. The Federation of Junior Colleges had signed a pact with the University of California not to pursue upward expansion, but legislators felt themselves under no such proscriptions, given the tight economic climate. Conversion of a junior college made profound fiscal sense within a constituency. Junior colleges were funded largely from local taxes. (Fully 67 percent of operating costs and 100 percent of capital improvement dollars came from local sources [Douglass 2000, 225].) In contrast, state colleges received most of their funding from the state, not the district. (Only 28 percent of operating costs and 0 percent of capital improvement monies came from local sources [Douglass 2000, 225].) Conversion into a state college was a superb way to shift higher education spending to the whole state, thus spreading out the burden.

It's no surprise, then, that in those years of erosion of the University of California's funding base and the challenge to its unique status, Sproul kept the Subject A Committee and Subject A Office busy with a series of further investigations into complaints about lapses in the University of California's normally high standards.[24] In spring of 1955, the Committee on Subject A met, and, again at Sproul's urging, investigated the widespread dissatisfaction with Subject A: the exam, the course, the Subject A office, and, most importantly, the students involved. As before, Professor Evans drafted the committee's response. It was a forceful defense of the Subject A exam and course: "From time to time there runs through the University community a rumor that the Subject A exam and curriculum are inadequate. The Committee on Subject A emphatically denies that either the exam or the course is inadequate so far as its proper and limited function is concerned." He insisted that the Committee on Educational Policy and Sproul recognize the error of expecting Subject A to make the university safe from students' poor writing forevermore. "The 'Pass' grade in Subject A . . . indicates no more than that a student has demonstrated proficiency in written English appropriate to the high school graduation/college entrance level."[25]

Evans reiterated the argument that he had made earlier, in favor of junior-level instruction in writing. "The Committee on Subject A believes the University to be in error in supposing that Subject A will have seen to it that freshmen will, four years later, write like proper seniors." "Subject A instruction," Evans argued, "is incapable of performing miracles. It can and does require a standard of writing appropriate to college entrance. It cannot, through the same . . . course materials, maintain a standard appropriate for college graduation."[26] He reinstated the earlier recommendation of the Committee on Subject A that all students, junior college transfers and Berkeley students, take an exam in writing proficiency at the beginning of their junior years, and, if necessary, be required to take instruction.

It fell to Professor Connick, Committee on Educational Policy chair, to respond to Evans's letter. Connick had been chair in 1951, when the administration had so soundly rebuffed the proposal of a junior-level exam. He replied to Evans, "The Committee on Educational Policy has had a very heavy agenda and could not address the . . . proposal regarding upper-division students' writing."[27] Connick assured the Subject A Committee that the proposal would be passed on to the incoming chair of the Committee on Educational Policy.

In the new academic year, the reconstituted Committee on Educational Policy considered the Subject A Committee's proposal. Like their predecessors, they acknowledged the role that every department has in composition improvement, but they articulated this role as one of enforcement rather than instruction: "This is not to say that every teacher should take time from his subject matter to give training in prose composition, [b]ut if today and every day the student were faced with an unremitting demand in all his written work for clear, grammatical English, and *penalized for* the lack of it, undergraduate illiteracy would disappear" (emphasis in original).[28]

Like their predecessors, the Committee on Educational Policy endorsed heartily the proposal for a junior year exam[29] Mindful, no doubt, of the administration's strong resistance to calling into question junior college students' prior training, the committee made the point that it was necessary to test Berkeley juniors ("natives") as well, "to avoid the appearance of setting up special hurdles for transfer students."[30] This proposal evidently met some hurdles of its own; no action was taken.

The following year the Committee on Educational Policy addressed the continuing chorus of complaint about students' writing by asking the Subject A Committee to consider making proficiency in Subject A an entrance requirement. The Subject A Committee's deliberation reflected an acute awareness of enrollment pressures in 1956, when 2724 freshmen were admitted.[31] The Subject A exam had long been a placement test designed to sort students who had already been accepted into the university. The Committee on Subject A recognized that, as an entrance exam, the Subject A examination would become "a means of decreasing the size of the under-graduate student body."[32] The committee also quickly saw that the Subject A Office would become, in effect, a division of the Office of Admissions.

Subject A Committee Chair Professor James Lynch, disquieted at the prospect of this new role of "check[ing] the unlimited growth of under-graduate enrollment," reminded his committee of the merits of its earlier proposal for a junior-level exam in writing proficiency. Retaining the Subject A exam's status as a sorting exam for admitted freshmen and in-stituting a junior-level exam would have the benefit, Lynch argued, "of screening out or holding back those unable to pursue further University study, in accord with the University's most effective employment of funds and facilities." Such a two-stage writing examination process would have the effect, he maintained, of "keeping the student body as a whole aware that the University expects that improvement in language ability will ac-company a growing acquaintance with knowledge of all kinds."[33]

Lynch's contention that students' ability to write about a subject de-velops simultaneously with their deepening engagement with the subject material echoed the Prose Improvement Project's core refrain. But it fell on deaf ears.

The Subject A Committee's other members reminded Lynch that "un-dergraduate enrollments, especially in the first two years, would have to be severely restricted."[34] Willing to accept a role in the admissions process, they outvoted him. With Lynch dissenting, the committee recommended that the Subject A exam be made an entrance exam as soon as possible. The Committee on Educational Policy took up this recommendation at the beginning of the next academic year, eventually submitting to Chan-cellor Kerr its endorsement of the proposal to use the Subject A exam for admissions decisions. It also proposed the institution of a junior-level writ-ing exam. The administration supported neither of these proposals.

The implementation of either proposal would carry substantial polit-ical consequences for the University of California, of course. Tightened admissions standards based in part upon Subject A exam scores would re-sult in a freshman class more proficient in writing, and would help to counter the deleterious effects of enrollment pressures. However, tight-ened standards would also send more students to the state colleges. Sproul and Kerr were still fighting the growth of the state colleges, still arguing to the legislature that no more state colleges needed to be built, that existing state colleges need not be expanded. And while instituting a junior-level writing exam at the university would improve the quality of students' writing in the upper division, and at graduation, and thus would improve the university's reputation among employers, it stood to alienate the junior colleges, whose support the university needed most desperately in its fight to restrain the development of the state college system. Examining transfer students on the quality of the training in composition they had received at the junior college threatened the partnership that the university had nurtured with the junior colleges for twenty years.

In 1956 and 1957, higher education in California experienced two intensely difficult years. Again, the legislature questioned the need for California to maintain three separate types of institution (Douglass 2000, 230). Lawmakers were particularly attuned to the costliness of higher education in 1956 as the state entered into its first solid postwar recession, and as it absorbed 2.2 million Californians in another wave of in-migration (Douglass 2000, 230).

That year the legislature began scrutinizing the university's use of state funds, noting that the university received twice the amount of funding as the state colleges, but that the total enrollment of the state colleges was higher. In an atmosphere of increasing antipathy toward the university, a bill was proposed that would study the long-range financing of California's higher education and the kinds of institutions of higher education that Californians needed and wanted. Anticipating that the results of such a study would not be in the university's best interest, Sproul worked hard to get the bill defeated. He succeeded. The junior colleges did not fare as well. They were dealt a body blow in the legislature early in 1957 when the bill to increase their funding was defeated. There were quarrels among the three segments of higher education: public demands for increased enrollment and expanded programs mounted, and there was limited, and sometimes grudging, support in Sacramento. Yet again, the legislature wanted to know just what distinguished one segment of higher education from another (Douglass 2000, 230). As the biggest stakeholder of the three, the university had the most to lose.

Again, the pressure was on the university to distinguish itself from the others. Again, the "illiteracy of students" became one of the means through which the university could distinguish its standards from those of the other institutions.[35] Chancellor Kerr wrote to the Committee on Educational Policy, expressing his grave concerns that many of Berkeley students' prose failed to observe even "the decencies of English."[36] The College of Letters and Science readily seconded Kerr's concern, noting that the high standards of the college were being compromised "by the substantial number of new admits who have demonstrated an inability to write English with even modest facility."[37]

In April of 1957, the College of Letters and Science at UC Berkeley voted to regard the Subject A exam as an entrance exam for applicants to that college. The nature of the curriculum in Letters and Science, they reasoned, necessitated that students "be qualified *at the onset of their college program* to communicate what they know and what they think with reasonable proficiency" (emphasis in original).[38] Letters and Science Dean Fretter suggested at a meeting of the Academic Senate the following month that the entire campus would do well to adopt Subject A as an entrance requirement, so that the university's high standards would be protected in every department.

The proposal from the Letters and Science faculty met with opposition in the Academic Senate. The opposition, however, was not directed against the proposal of a Subject A entrance exam; rather, it was directed against what several members perceived as Letters and Science's misreading of the Subject A requirement.[39] They believed that Letters and Science had set standards too high. Senate regulations called for entrants to be able to "write English without gross errors in spelling, grammar, diction, and punctuation."[40] A "gross errors" bar was as much as could legally be asked from California's high school students by its university. Dean Fretter pointed out that the Subject A exam as presently administered called for substantially more than control over gross errors: "The current test is designed to supply evidence of the ability to communicate what students have learned and what they think with some reasonable proficiency."[41] Fretter argued further that mere avoidance of gross error could lead to cautious, oversimple prose that communicates little at all. In support of this view, he quoted the Subject A booklet for 1956: "A writer must have something to say if he is to write an acceptable composition. His writing should indicate that he has done some thinking."[42]

E. W. Strong, chair of the Committee on Educational Policy, and later chancellor of Berkeley, agreed with the College of Letters and Science that entering students should be required to prove themselves capable of producing "thoughtful, reasonably proficient prose" rather than merely able to "avoid gross error." However, as he argued in his report to Chancellor Kerr, the university was bound by its own regulations to apply the grosser gross-errors standard. He was particularly concerned to prevent the disunity that he believed would result if the College of Letters and Science applied different admission standards than did the other colleges. Strong's letter elided the fact that at that time several colleges did already apply separate entrance standards. For example, applicants to the College of Engineering had to take an Engineering Aptitude Test, and applicants to the College of Agriculture had to meet different requirements.

Kerr promptly appointed a Special Committee on Subject A to discuss the "problems allied" with Letters and Science's proposal. Members included representatives from the Office of Admissions, Office of Relations with Schools, College of Letters and Science, Committee on Educational Policy, and Subject A Committee. The members did not tarry over the questions that had interested Letters and Science and the Committee on Educational Policy. Taking it as a given that avoidance of gross error was the skill to be measured in Subject A, this Special Committee quickly moved on to an examination of the exam.

Like so many of the students, the exam failed miserably. The Special Committee found it to be "practically without value." The Special Committee scrutinized correlation studies, noting that one study, the "Duff Study" of 1945, showed only a weak correlation between the essay section of the exam and the objective section (Duff 1945, 19). They conceded that a second study did show a statistically significant relationship between students' scores on the Subject A exam and on the verbal portion of the SAT. This study the Special Committee dismissed as invalid because it was carried out in 1947, a period when the subjects were "presumably atypical veterans."[43] A third study showed that if the Subject A exam had been an entrance exam in 1951, some 25 percent of the students whom the university had accepted would have been denied admission. This denial, of course, would have been unthinkable in 1951, amidst postwar enrollment pressures and the encroachment of state colleges.

The fourth element of the Special Committee's indictment of the Subject A exam produced the most lively prose. This element also begins to explain why the colleges of Engineering and Agriculture could exact different entrance requirements without censure, while the College of Letters and Science could not: "Certain sex differences emerge," the committee suggested darkly. If the Subject A exam had been used as an admission exam in 1952, of male and female applicants with equal high school GPAs, 45 percent of the males would have to have been denied admission.[44]

The Special Committee's further discussion of this problem merits quotation at some length:

> Women traditionally do better in the Subject A exam while our male students are brighter on any type of general aptitude test. The reason for this relative brightness of men, incidentally, is that women are more predictable and work more nearly up to capacity, so that when both sexes must meet the same standard, as they must, to be eligible for the University, the men are automatically brighter . . . Any device that puts restrictions on the entrance of male students at the University of California should be looked at askance.[45]

And so it was. Not askance enough, however, to preclude the university from using the exam as a way to comment on the weakness of students it had already admitted, or of articulating the ways that students do not measure up to the high standards of the University of California.

Indeed, the Special Committee grasped the opportunity to declaim the rhetoric of remediation with particular flair in the conclusion of its report: "The English department should be thanked for its valiant and never-ending battle with the tides of the semi-literate welling up annually from the secondary schools."[46]

CHAPTER 7

"The Tides of the Semi-literate"

> The state college system was in a restless state and in high competition for expanding its base and upgrading its institutions to university status, and was posed to come into conflict with the University at every stage.
>
> *Kerr 2001, xxiii.*

THE FIRST TUESDAY of November 1957 was a great day for California Democrats. Edmund G. "Pat" Brown was elected governor, and for the first time in a hundred years, Democrats held the majority in both houses. Governor Brown was to prove himself an excellent friend of higher education, and a staunch supporter of Clark Kerr in times of trouble. Kerr had accepted the regents' offer of the presidency of the University of California upon Sproul's retirement in July, although he was not inaugurated until September of 1958. Governor-elect Brown was initially rather critical of the University of California, characterizing it as a "Republican institution" and "the wave of the past" (Kerr 2001, 161). He saw the state colleges as the more democratic (and Democratic) institutions, and more worthy of his support.[1] In January of 1958, as soon as the new legislature was convened, the Senate began hearings on the state of education in California. The Senate Investigative Committee on Education cited the need for "a reevaluation of the primary purposes, tools, and techniques of our public education program since the event of Sputnik."[2] This legislative committee, not surprisingly, found that one of the greatest problems plaguing public education in California was "lack of legislative influence" (Douglass 2000, 257).

The committee also faulted the administrations of each of the three segments of higher education for failure to coordinate their efforts. The university, the state colleges, and the junior colleges were expanding, adding programs, and setting admission standards without due regard for each other, or for the taxpayer, the Senate report complained. This duplication, or triplication, of missions could ill be tolerated in the time of Sputnik. President-elect Kerr had already turned his exceptional tactical gifts to the resolution of this problem. In November of 1957 he had submitted to the regents his Long-Range Development Program, designed to bring order to what he characterized as "chaos" (Kerr 2001, 156). He set out to find ways to induce the university, the state colleges, and the junior colleges "to move toward an orderly plan" (Douglass 2000, 257).

Particularly disorderly was the "growing political aggressiveness" (Kerr 2001, 179) of the state colleges in their pursuit of the PhD and the right to conduct research. The state colleges and their strong champions in the legislature had, of course, been pressing for upward expansion for some time. Sputnik's afterburn in Washington—zealous support for higher education, especially in its research functions—further inflamed the state colleges' ambitions: "All that federal R&D money was out there for the asking, and they [the state colleges] wanted their share of it," notes Kerr in his memoir (2001, 176). Kerr's memoir fails to make explicit what surely was the corollary ambition: the University of California was not about to relinquish any of its share of that federal R&D money without a fight.

Never so much a combatant as a conciliator, Kerr had already taken steps to acknowledge the state colleges as a critically important segment of higher education in California. Rather than fighting all legislation to expand existing state colleges or establish new ones, as Sproul had done, Kerr sought out concessions. This was particularly true in his negotiations with Glen Dumke, president of San Jose State College, and Malcolm Love, president of San Diego State College. Throughout 1958, these two men lobbied Sacramento hard for legislation that would enable them to offer graduate degrees in engineering and in education. Their choice to push for these two areas of graduate study was inspired strategy in that time of Sputnik. To vote against legislation that would help the U.S. catch up to the Russians in technology and education was tantamount to "jeopardiz[ing] CA's contribution to national defense" (Douglass 2000, 251). Kerr, shrewdly recognizing the power of this call to arms, pledged to support a graduate-level engineering program at San Jose State College. He also agreed to support a small research role—particularly research in education—for state college faculty (Douglass 2000, 257). In exchange for these concessions, the state colleges agreed with Kerr's assertion that higher education needed "to move toward an orderly plan" (Douglass 2000, 257). This plan was to become the blueprint differentiating the functions of the three segments of higher education.

By 1960, after intense and very complex political battles, this Master Plan for Higher Education was made law.[3] Under the Master Plan, the junior colleges were required to accept all of California's high school graduates. These open-access institutions were rechristened "community colleges," because they were to be sited within commuting distance of virtually all Californians. The plan projected the need for twenty-two new community colleges to be built throughout the state. New state colleges were to be built as well—two more in addition to the four already under construction. State colleges would be required to accept the top 33.3 percent of all high school graduates (rather than the 50–60 percent they had accepted prior to 1960). The University of California was to lay claim to the top 12.5 percent of high school graduates (rather than the 15 percent it had accepted prior to 1960). Plans were underway for three more University of California campuses. Transfer provisions among the three segments were to be articulated.

A further, and critical, provision of the Master Plan reserved to the university the right to grant the PhD, as well as degrees in medicine and law. The state colleges were to be permitted to offer the MA degree and certain professional degrees in engineering. The university, and not the state colleges, was to be California's only research institution, although state college faculty were to be permitted to pursue limited research roles.

Additionally, the Master Plan called for the state colleges to enjoy the same public-trust status that the university had under the California constitution. Public trust status, it will be remembered, guaranteed the university a substantial measure of protection from legislative intervention. That is, while the legislature held the right and responsibility to oversee the university's budget as a whole, it did not have license to draft the budget itself or to control discrete elements of it. That right was held by the regents, in concert with the university's president. The public-trust status held by the university was very much coveted by the state colleges, the budgets of which were susceptible to intense legislative tinkering. The Master Plan proposed to extend that desirable status to the state colleges, but this provision of the legislation was eliminated. The state colleges never attained public trust status.

Overall, Kerr's Master Plan can be seen as a remarkably successful strategy of containment. Formalizing the role of the state colleges, identifying them as state universities, fixing their place in the tripartite system, would bring to a halt their expansion upward. The Master Plan would also check the attempt of any state college legislatively to elbow its way into the university system (as Santa Barbara had done). The Master Plan wisely allowed for lateral expansion; it allowed the state colleges to develop a range of programs offering certification at the MA or MS level. However, by blocking any program development beyond that level, Kerr's Master Plan confirmed the role of the state colleges—each institution now a member of the California State University system—as "polytechnic institutions" (Kerr 2001, 186). And it reaffirmed these institutions' long-held role as a teachers' colleges. Kerr shrugs off charges that he struck a "thieves' bargain" or that the university "won the whole thing" (2001, 184), but it cannot be denied that the Master Plan put the university solidly, profoundly, publicly, on top.

The Master Plan was a triumph rhetorically, as well. It put California in the vanguard of John F. Kennedy's New Frontier, raising the ante on the American Dream. The shining American principle of *mass* access to higher education paled next to the shimmering Californian principle of *universal* access.[4] The sunny republic stunned the country by boldly surfing the tidal wave of young people clamoring for higher education, offering a place to every graduate that her high schools produced.

President Kerr made the cover of *Time*'s October 17, 1960 issue in a story called "Master Planner," and California's story of the systematization and accessibility of her higher education brought respect surging back to a university laid low by the ravages of the loyalty oath controversy. Kerr's Master Plan was hailed as a "distinctive effort to reconcile patriotism with elitism" (Kerr 2001, 187). This was no small achievement in what had by then become the nation's second-most populous state. Kerr remembers that period as a golden age for the university, and particularly for Berkeley, which he heralded as "the Harvard of the West" (2001, 347), and "the great rising star in the firmament of universities nationwide and even worldwide" (2001, 156).

A star may have been born with the Master Plan, but there were still more ideas twinkling in the regents' eyes. Very quickly, plans were conceived for three additional campuses. With more than fifty thousand students—all qualified under the 12.5 percent rule of the Master Plan—clamoring for places, this star would "soon be sharing its privileges with eight siblings," fretted Kerr (2001, 348).

Berkeley was willing enough to share the undergraduate load, but it jealously guarded its graduate training and research functions (Kerr 2001, 350). UCLA was similarly possessive. It had fought difficult battles with Berkeley, both academic and political, to get its share of status. It wasn't until the postwar boom, beginning in the late 1940s, that Berkeley wholly yielded to UCLA's demands for full graduate training and research functions.

Berkeley's resistance to confirming additional siblings as research universities was particularly intense in the early 1960s, when federal funding was flowing to research universities in the hundreds of millions (Kerr 2001). The rising star was reluctant to be just one element of a constellation of Universities of California. Having finally thwarted the aspirations of the state colleges, Berkeley now had to hold the line against upstart new branches of the university. Smelser (1974) observes that Berkeley's resistance took the form of opposition to any moves to centralize decision-making functions and faculty authority, or to regularize procedures across campuses. Berkeley stood in relation to the other campuses of the university as the university as a whole stood in relation to the state colleges (Smelser 1974, 76).

Kerr reports "hard feelings" among UC Berkeley's faculty at the diversion of wealth to other UC campuses, particularly the diversion of federal research dollars. Throughout the decade, Berkeley was to see its resource base and its powers erode as the University of California strained to become the nation's first "multiversity" (Kerr's coinage). As much as Kerr insists that the enactment of the Master Plan was UC Berkeley's shining moment, affirmation of its status as the jewel in the crown, he concedes in his recent memoir also that "it was a traumatic transition" for the campus (2001, 156).[5]

California was herself working through the trauma of redefinition in those years. From 1958 to 1966, Governor Pat Brown pursued a broad policy of social reform, expanding the social welfare system, increasing aid to schools, developing the state's infrastructure, pressing for consumer-protection legislation, and supporting higher education. At the same time, the John Birch Society was sinking its roots deep in California soil; legislation to ban racial discrimination in housing was being castigated as an attack on homeowners' rights (Beck and Williams 1972); the Red-hunting Joint Fact-Finding Committee on Un-American Activities had been reincarnated under the leadership of State Senator Hugh Burns of Los Angeles, successor to Senator Tenney in this crusade. Kerr characterizes California of this period as "a state with elements of political instability (right and left) beyond those in other states" (2001, 166).

The Burns committee had earlier identified Kerr as "a possible undercover communist" who was "to be neutralized in his job or even dismissed" (Rosenfeld 2002). In 1959, the University of California's putative Redness drew the ire of J. Edgar Hoover himself. FBI Director Hoover was a famously busy man in those particularly chilly days of the cold war, but apparently he found time to peruse the topics for the University of California's Subject A examination.

There, among topics such as

> If you could live in a time and place other than your own, what time and place would you choose? Why?

and

> It seems that the star athlete is no longer the high school hero he was a few years ago. By whom has he been replaced (if by anyone)? What do you think accounts for this change?

Director Hoover encountered the following topic:

> What are the dangers to a democracy of a national police organization,
>   like the FBI, which operates secretly and is unresponsive to public
>   criticism?[6]

The Subject A archives do not indicate how many of the 1,040 students who took the exam that year chose to write to that topic, nor, sadly, were any specimen essays retained. Thus, it is not clear whether any young minds were turned un-American by the Subject A exam. Still, a high-placed priest in the Los Angeles archdiocese spoke out against this Subject A exam topic, as did the head of the International Association of Chiefs of Police. Both men were mindful, perhaps, of the risks spelled out in a 1959 House Un-American Activities Committee Publication, "Language as a Communist Weapon." Hoover spoke to Governor Brown, and Governor Brown spoke to the regents; the regents withdrew the exam topic and affirmed their highest regard for the FBI. The sixty-page report sent to Hoover from the California offices of the FBI described the Subject A exam topic as "merely one example of the deterioration of the morality and patriotism of this great university" (Rosenfeld 2002). The FBI launched a search for the contributor of that Subject A topic, and they identified Professor Everett Jones from UCLA. Both Professor Jones and Mrs. Jones were reported to UCLA Chancellor Knudson as "fanatical adherents to communism," Professor Jones having "inherited leftist sympathies from his father, a Unitarian minister" (Rosenfeld 2002).

UCLA's Chancellor Knudson took no action against Jones's genes, which is just as well, because the FBI later discovered that it was actually Berkeley's own Professor James Lynch who had authored the offending topic. This discovery led to the inclusion of seventy-two members of the Berkeley faculty and senior administration on the FBI Security Index. The Security Index was a list of persons whom the FBI considered political threats; in the event of a crisis, these persons were to be detained indefinitely, without warrant, on Angel Island, in the San Francisco Bay (Rosenfeld 2002).

Professor Lynch was never detained on Angel Island. Neither was he dismissed from his post, nor even disbarred from the Subject A Committee. In 1961, the year that the U.S. and the USSR each resumed nuclear weapons testing, and the year of John F. Kennedy's Bay of Pigs Invasion, the list of Subject A exam topics included the following

> Arming to protect peace cannot help but produce war. Discuss and evalu-
> ate this statement. (Subject A Archives)

This topic would seem at least as provocative of thought—and FBI response—as that earlier one, but it did not attract fire from Director Hoover, the International Chiefs of Police, or the bishopric of Southern California. Perhaps this is because in 1961, Subject A examinees were being held to different, less probing, levels of engagement with their thoughts. Swept away were the examiner's injunctions that "[a student's] writing should indicate that he has done some thinking" and "[A] writer must have something to say . . ."[7] These liberal, possibly even Unitarian, rubrics were firmly replaced with the advice that a passing exam is "correct," "co-herent," and "reasonably free of spelling, diction, sentence structure, and punctuation errors."[8]

Again, sadly, no samples of students' essays could be located, nor could a count of the students who responded to this topic. It seems quite likely that this topic had few takers.

A cohort of eighteen-year-olds trained as schoolchildren to "duck and cover," very likely saw "arming to protect peace" as an uncontroversial article of faith, rather than as a subject for their critical scrutiny.

The 1961 exam offered students the following, perhaps more attrac-tive, alternative:

> Each of the following terms has been applied to the age we live in: the
> Age of Anxiety, the Age of Analysis, the Age of Foam Rubber.
> Choose the term which you think is most appropriate and explain
> why you think it suits our times.[9]

By that time, whatever anxiety Director Hoover felt about the University of California had shifted far away from the Subject A examination. The FBI had trained its energies on more troubling aspects of the Red University. In May of 1960, the House Un-American Activities Committee had come to San Francisco to conduct hearings of the Americanness of certain Northern Californians. On May 13, the opening day of the hearings, a few hundred people, many of them UC Berkeley students, gathered at City Hall chambers to demonstrate against the hearings. The City Hall demonstrations, and especially Berkeley students' participation in them, inspired the FBI to publish a special report, "Communist Target—Youth:

Communist Infiltration and Agitation Tactics," claiming that a UC Berkeley student had "provided the spark that touched off the flame of violence" (Rosenfeld 2002).

There was, in fact, not much violence in that initial fracas, and any spark was soon dowsed by the fire hoses that turned City Hall's marble steps into waterfalls and washed the building clean of demonstrators. Thirty-one UC Berkeley students were arrested,[10] and the following day, some five thousand demonstrators arrived at City Hall to conduct a far more strenuous demonstration against the House Un-American Activities Committee (Rorabaugh 1989). The San Francisco offices of the FBI likened the demonstration to the 1934 Waterfront Strike, the raucous dispute led by activist and likely communist Harry Bridges that shut down the western seaboard (Rorabaugh 1989). The FBI report included the following advisory to Director Hoover: "What is particularly significant and undoubtedly of interest to you is that much of the manpower for this riotous situation was provided by the University of California at Berkeley" (Rosenfeld 2002).

The FBI report was of interest to the host of television's *GE Theater*, who wanted to make "Communist Target—Youth" into a TV program. Hoover wasn't thinking Hollywood, though, and the phone calls from the host of *GE Theater* went unreturned. It would be a few more years before Hoover began returning calls from Ronald Reagan. By the middle of the decade, when gubernatorial candidate Reagan pledged "to purge UC Berkeley of beatniks, radicals, and filthy speech advocates"(Rosenfeld 2002), he had Director Hoover's rapt attention.

But this is to move ahead of the story. In the early 1960s, UC Berkeley was still in the period that Clark Kerr characterized as its "golden age" (2001, 56). Labor-economist Kerr interpreted his job as manager of this new creation, the multiversity, and saw that this management entailed recasting university administrators into professional managers (Rorabaugh 1989), and bringing the university's tradition of a liberal arts curriculum into harmony with the realities of post-Sputnik higher education. Like California herself, UC Berkeley had been radically re-formed by World War II, and its dependence upon government-sponsored research continued in the sixties, when Berkeley had closer ties to the federal government than any other university (Kerr 2002). Additionally, Berkeley maintained a different kind of tie to the federal government in those years, when it sent forth more Peace Corps volunteers than any other university or college.

In the spring of 1962, President Kennedy came to campus to deliver the Charter Day address. The Greek Theater swelled with an audience of eighty-eight thousand, reportedly the largest number of people ever to assemble to hear Kennedy speak (Rorabaugh 1989). The fall of that same year brought the Cuban Missile Crisis, and some fifteen hundred Berkeley students and professors gathered at the junction of Telegraph and Bancroft Avenues to debate Kennedy's brinksmanship. It was a small crowd, but a significant moment; this was the first time since World War II that this campus, with its intimate connection to the federal government, had questioned U.S. foreign policy (Rorabaugh 1989).

The junction of Telegraph and Bancroft had been a site of political activity since the early 1930s, when President Sproul banned political speech on campus.[11] In the early 1960s, students and others involved in the civil rights movement set up tables on that corner, from which they distributed leaflets and collected donations. Guided by the same sense of idealism that inspired so many Berkeley students to join the Peace Corps, some sixty Berkeley students had spent the summer of 1964 in Mississippi working on voter registration drives (Rorabaugh 1989).

That summer, it will be remembered, was a tense time for race relations in America. Race riots had erupted in several major cities, including New York and Chicago, as well as in smaller eastern towns. San Francisco did not see rioting, although the Republican National Convention, held that year in San Francisco, was disrupted by anti-Goldwater demonstrators, many of them Berkeley students protesting Goldwater's hostility to the civil rights movement. The Congress of Racial Equality held demonstrations against discrimination in housing and employment at a number of San Francisco locations, and, indeed, in the city of Berkeley. In 1963 Berkeley city voters had defeated an open-housing ordinance, insisting that such a regulation trod on homeowners' rights, and the following year, many students participated in protests against alleged hiring discrimination at a Lucky's Supermarket a few blocks from campus on Telegraph Avenue (Rorabaugh 1989).

In those highly charged early years of the decade, an increasing number of students were drawn to political activity. The civil rights movement was the impetus, but soon other groups found voice. Gradually, the political activity moved onto campus, and tables were set up on Sproul Plaza. In September of 1964, in consultation with neither President Kerr nor Chancellor Strong, the vice chancellor for student affairs had these groups forcibly removed from campus.

This action and the subsequent student—and later, faculty—resistance to it brought on the free speech movement. A protracted series of physical skirmishes between students and police, procedural skirmishes between faculty and administration, and political skirmishes between President Kerr and the regents, the free speech movement was the first large-scale campus disruption in the U.S. A harbinger.[12] With its sit-ins, near-daily rallies, occupations of campus buildings, mass arrests (the largest in California's history),[13] boycotts of classes, and student strikes, the free speech movement was Clark Kerr's undoing. He lost the confidence of his faculty, who voted 824 to 115 against him and in support of the free speech movement leaders' demands; he lost the confidence of the regents, who ratified the faculty vote. "The result was almost incredible," one historian of the free speech movement remarks; "a handful of civil rights activists energized a large number of students, persuaded a recalcitrant faculty to accept their position, and went on to gain the support of the wealthiest and most powerful men in the state of California. The Free Speech Movement changed the University" (Rorabaugh 1989, 37).

The complicated and compelling story of the free speech movement is central to any history of UC Berkeley, and to any study of the rhetoric of student activism of the sixties.[14] The free speech movement is, however, not central to my story of the rhetoric of remediation at Berkeley. The students most passionately engaged in the free speech movement, those eight hundred who were dragged by an army of police officers out of the Administration Building, were not the kind of students who were "held" for Subject A. These protesters maintained above-average GPAs; they were English majors, history and philosophy majors (Muscatine 1968). They more than likely had passed their Subject A exam, the older students presumably having written without gross error on the "Age of Foam Rubber," the younger ones having successfully expressed their views on the "Value of the Future Farmers of America" (a 1963 Subject A exam topic). Still and all, the free speech movement and the students involved in it figure into my story because they became the lens through which could be focused a new wave of complaint about the problems of the university and the unsuitability of its students. More than anyone else, Reagan helped Californians focus their complaints. Central to his campaign strategy was his promise, oft-repeated, that he would "clean up the mess at UC Berkeley," and his frequently aired comment that he was "sorry that they did away with paddles in fraternities" (Rosenfeld 2002).

In fact, by 1965, they might as well have done away with fraternities themselves. Interest in Greek life and the sort of social activities that had characterized their parents' collegiate days was greatly diminished. Indeed, many of these students' parents had not had collegiate days. Between the end of the 1950s and the middle of the 1960s, the composition of Berkeley's student body changed substantially. Undergraduate enrollment leapt by 40 percent in just four years, between 1960 and 1964 (Rorabaugh 1989). Of freshmen admitted in 1959, 43 percent reported that their fathers were Republican, 34 percent Democrat.[15] Some 55 percent reported that they were Protestant, 11 percent Catholic.[16] By 1966, the demographics stacked up differently: 45 percent of freshmen reported that Dad was a Democrat, 33 percent a Republican. Only 39 percent were Protestant, while the percentage of Catholics had risen to 18 percent. In 1966, a full 27 percent reported that their background was "not religious," a huge change from 1959, when only 6 percent reported that they came from a nonreligious home. Perhaps most interesting was the fact that in 1966, some 31 percent of freshmen reported that at least one of their parents was foreign born. (All statistics in this section are from Rorabaugh [1989].) No parallel data on parents' national origins are reported for the 1959 survey; either the figure was insignificant, or the question not asked.

Ronald Reagan had another question to ask, and he asked it in as many speeches as he could in his run for the State House: "Will we allow a great University to be brought to its knees by a noisy, dissident minority?" (Rosenfeld 2002). Candidate Reagan delivered himself of a white-paper report charging President Kerr with promoting an "anything-goes atmosphere that has turned the University into a haven for protestors and sex deviants" (Rosenfeld 2002). Reagan defeated Pat Brown in a landslide, and warned students in his inaugural address, "Observe the rules or get out!" (Dalleck 1999, 39). Very quickly Governor Reagan's plans to cut the budget for higher education and to impose tuition on University of California students for the first time in its history were leaked to the press.

These plans engendered a strong new wave of student protests, this time with Reagan burned in effigy, more demonstrations, rallies, and marches. These protests were met with arrests, imposition of martial law (at the governor's request), shots being fired into crowds of student demonstrators, and tear-gassing from National Guard helicopters. Before Reagan's first month as governor was out, President Kerr had been dismissed. Reagan denied requests from both the mayor and the chancellor to rescind martial law, but he did agree to a gradual reduction of National Guard forces. By Memorial Day, the siege had ended. Reagan had proved that he was "dedicated to the destruction of disruptive elements on California campuses" (Rosenfeld 2002). By Reagan's lights, primary among those disruptive elements to be destroyed was Clark Kerr himself. Kerr's—and Berkeley's—golden age was over.

CHAPTER 8

"Viewed as Disgraceful by Many Scholars"

By 1969 most members of the university
were angry and exhausted, almost shell
shocked. Radical graffiti, spilled garbage
cans, false fire alarms, and stink bombs
formed a tedious routine punctuated only
by an occasional sit-in, disrupted class, or
sound of a rock breaking a window . . .
Cautious professors put masking tape on
the glass in their office doors . . . [and] the
senseless, random nature of the violent at-
tacks pained and puzzled the faculty who
increasingly came to see the protestors in
pathological terms.

Rorabaugh 1989, 161.

IT WAS NOT JUST the protestors who were pathologized in the second half
of that volatile decade at Berkeley. Students who failed the Subject A exam
were, once again, submitted to a range of diagnoses. In 1965, Chancellor
Kerr had proposed that the Subject A course be dissolved and these students be admitted into a "writing clinic."[1] He had earlier proposed alternative treatments for Subject A maladies, such as recorded TV lectures and
lab work with audio tapes.[2]

In those years of generalized public outrage about the state of affairs
at UC Berkeley—not to mention the state of emergency—there were,
as well, many complaints about Subject A from members of the general
public, from parents and students, and from high school teachers and
administrators.[3] One strongly critical letter from a well-placed parent
prompted Vice President Angus Taylor to charge the university-wide
Committee on Educational Policy with conducting a "comprehensive ex-

amination" of the Subject A requirement to see if it was "well justified," or if it should be abolished. Taylor asked the committee to consider the Subject A exam, as well, to determine if it should be redesignated an entrance exam. Expressing President Kerr's wish as well as his own, he wrote the committee chair: "We invite you and your committee to take a fresh and hard look at Subject A."[4]

Among the experts taking a fresh and hard look was E. J. Knapton, supervisor of Subject A at Berkeley, who addressed himself to the proposal of making Subject A an entrance exam. One problem with the proposal, Knapton suggested, is that it would discriminate against students "from relatively poor high schools, notably, but not exclusively the rural schools."[5] It is a debatable claim that in 1966, California's poorer high schools were primarily in rural, and not urban areas. It is unarguable, however, that students from rural schools, less affected by the upheavals in the cities during those years of the civil rights movement,[6] would have been seen as a potentially stabilizing element of the student body in 1965, and thus not an element to be discriminated against.

Knapton's more compelling adumbration was the claim that if Subject A were an admissions exam, the freshman class would be 75 percent female, and that some departments would have no new enrollments.[7] The Committee on Educational Policy took this dire warning to heart, as had their predecessors in 1958, and reported to Vice President Taylor: "Passing the Subject A examination cannot be made an admissions requirement without changing the composition of the student body, very possibly not for the better."[8]

The following year, the complaint about Subject A came from less exalted offices, but with rather more rhetorical force. Professor Samuel Markowitz, of the Chemistry Department, took a juridical turn, insisting that "the CEP show cause why the exam in Subject A and the course in Subject A should not be abolished."[9] Markowitz asked, "What other University has such an exam and course?" Arguing that the proficiency level certified by Subject A was wholly the responsibility of the high schools, he professed that venerable—if not outright shopworn—conviction that "with reasonable lead time" the high schools would shoulder their rightful burden. "Here," pointed Markowitz, "is an opportunity to assert our standards."[10]

The Committee on Educational Policy chose not to seize that opportunity. Rather, they referred in their letter of response to the spotty record of the high schools in producing graduates with Subject A proficiency. Professor Wayne Shumaker, for example, detailed his impressions of English instruction at McClymonds High in Oakland. He observed that students' learning activities centered about reading a Clorox bleach pamphlet on cleaning clothing, and reading a set of instructions on tooth brushing.[11] Asserting the university's standards by making Subject A an entrance exam, Committee on Educational Policy Chair Pimentel explained, would have the effect of reducing the freshman class by 50 percent,[12] and UC Berkeley could not afford to do that; enrollment pressures were too high. The students had to be accommodated somehow. "The only thing we could do," mused Pimentel, "is lower our Pass standards and admit the same number of students we now admit," an option he considered unacceptable.[13]

Finally, the Committee on Educational Policy's response dealt the coup de grâce to Markowitz's "show cause" demand: use of the Subject A exam as an admissions tool would result in a large increase in the number of females accepted. Warned Pimentel, "Some majors would be starved for students, while others would be overwhelmed with females."[14] It is not known whether the predicted apocalypse of starvation silenced Markowitz, or the prospect of being overwhelmed with females, but he was not heard to raise these demands again.

By 1967, the demographics of UC Berkeley were beginning to shift again. The tidal wave of 1960–64, each year of which brought a thousand additional freshmen to Berkeley,[15] had ebbed. Most of these students had already graduated, or left school. The boom from 1967 to 1970 was in students of Asian ancestry. The Asian American Studies Program had recently been established, and was part of the Ethnic Studies Department, which itself was born of the strife and spirit of the sixties, and of the activism of the Third World Liberation Front.

The Asian American Studies Program proposed a course, Asian Studies 3, specifically tailored to the needs of Asian American students who had yet to satisfy the Subject A requirement. That program had earlier lodged some complaints about the culturally insensitive treatment of Asian-ancestry students in Subject A classes, and the course proposal for AS 3 included goals of "building self-confidence" and "promoting spontaneity," along with developing composing skills.[16] The Committee on Educational Policy's Committee on Remedial Education, to whom the proposal made its way, solicited the views of the Subject A Program's Acting Supervisor Myrsam Wicksman about the course proposal and the complaints of cultural insensitivity in the Subject A program.

Wicksman's response served to support the course proposal, and to underscore doubts about his own faculty's effectiveness with nonwhite students. His letter to the committee noted, "We have enrolled in Subject A increasing numbers of Asian immigrants who are writing above the level at which they may be placed in [courses for] 'English for Foreign Students,' but who are still quite deficient with respect to college-level English composition." Wicksman's letter went on to comment on "the tendency of many Asian American students to write perfunctory, relatively underdeveloped essays and also a reluctance to take a strong position in an argumentative essay." He reported noticing among the Subject A faculty that he supervised "a kind of attitudinal behavior that makes a barrier to effective communication between many of our Asian American students and their Subject A instructors, because they are White."[17]

Faculty and subsequent Subject A supervisors were to dispute these claims about the students and these charges about the faculty's effectiveness. Additionally, they questioned Wicksman's judgment.[18] They may well have had reason to. Wicksman's letter to the committee had conflated the group "Asian immigrant students," whom he judged to be just barely proficient enough to be placed in courses other than "English for Foreign Students," with the group "Asian Americans," whose argumentation skills were weak. This conflation suggests that he was somewhat removed from even a basic understanding of these two very different populations. He may also have been at a correlate remove from his faculty's classroom practices. At any rate, the charges against the Subject A faculty were not further explored at that time,[19] nor were the doubts that had been expressed by the Committee on Courses about the confidence-building aims of the proposed Asian American Studies composition course. Responding to Committee on Courses Chair Professor Dekker's doubts, Brendan O'Hehir, chair of the Committee on Educational Policy-Remedial Education, conceded that he, too, was reluctant for the university to grant credit for "courses which duplicate high school work," but then reminded Dekker of the need for "recognizing the special circumstances that have led to these proposals," and for attaining the goals of Subject A-level instruction "without discrimination."[20]

Discussions of the matter continued through the next year, when Kim Newman, herself an instructor in the Subject A Program, accused the Subject A Program in general and its supervisor, Sabina Johnson, in particular, of racism toward Asian-ancestry students.[21] Johnson responded to this allegation with a measured, detailed, and convincing exegesis of the Subject A Program's aims, materials, procedures, and results.[22] Dean Knight found Johnson and the Subject A Program to be "unexceptionable," and indicated that he "would like to extend support, morally and otherwise, to Johnson and her staff."[23]

He *would* have liked to, but, Dean Knight went on to explain, "I find myself in a difficult situation. I do not want to stand in the way of any legitimate aspirations and complaints that the minority opponents of the [Subject A] program might have." Knight went on to reflect upon the sensitivity of "relations between the Subject A Program and various agencies of the Third World, particularly the Department of Ethnic Studies and the Educational Opportunity Program."[24]

Even amidst the birthing of cultural and identity politics at Berkeley that was occurring in those years, the faculty and administration of Asian American Studies and the Educational Opportunity Program might have been startled to think of themselves as "agencies of the Third World." They did, however, stand behind the complaint that the Subject A Program "force[d] minority students into patterns of thinking and writing which are calculated to compromise their cultural loyalties." The Asian American Studies composition course was approved, and UC Berkeley therewith endorsed the proposition that "it should be possible for minority group members to satisfy their English deficiencies through a program controlled by the Department of Ethnic Studies."[25]

At the same time that the Berkeley campus's Committee on Educational Policy was approving this course, the Academic Council for the whole of the University of California was again launching an inquiry into the utility of the Subject A requirement, and the validity of its objectives. Each campus was asked to appoint a committee to "consider possible alternatives to the Subject A requirement and course."[26] The result of this inquiry was the July 7, 1972 report to the University-wide Committee on Educational Policy by Ralph Turner, chair of the University-wide Committee on Educational Policy, and Jay Martin, Chair of the Committee on Educational Policy at UC Irvine, colloquially known as the "Turner-Martin Report." This report offered a brief but excellent history of the Subject A requirement, capturing the central paradox:

> One inevitable result of the University's generally admirable admission standards—not to speak of the recent abandonment of those standards—is the admission each year of many students who are unable to write a straightforward, literate answer to an essay examination in any college course.[27]

The Turner-Martin Report recapped the various expectations that had been attached to the Subject A requirement over the years: that students' writing should "be free of gross errors"; "be above the primer level"; "have developed, unified, and coherent paragraphing"; "attain a definable competency level"; and so forth. Each of these expectations is, of course, tied to a pedagogic moment, and the whole provides a wholly serviceable short course in composition history. The Turner-Martin Report made its own contribution to that history, fixing itself to the early 1970s by positing its own expectation:

> The Subject A requirement must be regarded as a guarantee that, at admission, or as shortly as possible thereafter, all students will be able to operate comfortably and successfully in what might be called "Standard Academic English."[28]

"Standard English" is, of course, a construct that has long been heavily freighted, but it is weighed down with vastly different baggage today— thirty years after the Turner-Martin Report—than it was by the things it carried in 1972.[29] Similarly time sensitive is the Turner-Martin Report's praise of the Subject A requirement and course for the "great educational contribution it makes toward improving the ability of a third of the students to use the language of their country."[30] In 1972, that "third" would have been black (12 percent), Asian (9 percent), and Chicano/a (7 percent) at UC Berkeley (Subject A Archives). Thus, the report's making reference to "the language of their country" seems somehow to be both invective and invitation.

That mixed message, of course, is in the very nature of the Subject A requirement. By the end of the report, the authors had reaffirmed the "high value and utility" of the Subject A requirement and course; recommended that the cost of teaching it be borne by the university, not the Subject A students themselves (a practice that began in 1922); and that baccalaureate credit—and not just workload credit—be granted for the nonremedial aspects of instruction. Not only should Subject A *not* be abolished or used as an entrance exam, the report asserted, the role it fills is "essential to the conduct of public education in a democratic society."[31]

Richard Donovan (1978) reminds us that public education at the postsecondary level is intensely vulnerable to market/enrollment pressures, and this was certainly the case at the University of California, obliged as it was by the Master Plan to embrace the top 12.5 percent of California's high school seniors who applied for admission. The Turner-Martin Report is mindful of this when it argues that using the Subject A exam for admissions in 1972 would have reduced the freshman class by 35–40 percent, many of these students "from culturally and economically deprived backgrounds," and points out that "[the university] is unlikely to turn away 35 to 40 percent of the number it now admits."[32]

Finally, the Turner-Martin Report takes the familiar rhetorical turn. The opportunity to assert the university's standards cannot be forgone: the university must, of course, accept, even welcome, these students, and provide for their academic needs—including Subject A instruction. But it cannot be denied that their level of English proficiency "is viewed as disgraceful by many scholars."[33]

The Subject A student, once again, embraced and disgraced.

Three years later, in 1975, the University of California went through yet another round of "reassessing the status and goals of Subject A," deciding, among other things, whether it should be used as an entrance exam. This subcommittee emerged with essentially the same recommendations as had its predecessors: Subject A cannot be abolished or made an entrance exam because the university is, after all, a public institution: "It has an obligation—practical as well as ethical—to provide the assistance that these students need."[34]

Professor Isaac, a member of the subcommittee, went a bit further in articulating the university's worries as well as its duties: "As long as we admit these students [who have yet to satisfy the Subject A requirement], let us recognize this deficiency as a reality of American culture."[35] Isaac wasn't alone in thinking of the writing problems of American eighteen-year-olds as a cultural epiphenomenon. Throughout the decade, the press grieved the decline in the literacy of those who would lay claim to a college education. In its issue of December 21, 1971, the *San Francisco Chronicle* asked,

> Why read at all, when all you need are "huh" and "far out" and "right on" to get you through the business of the day? When paragraphs have become grunts, what's the goal of searching out the pleasures of Lamb and Hazlitt? . . . The deprivation of public life revealed by Watergate [is] shown in language equally depraved.

At the end of 1975, *Newsweek* wondered in a cover story "Why Johnny Can't Write" (Sheils 1975) setting off a plague of jeremiads from, among others, the *New York Times*, the *Chicago Tribune*, the *Saturday Review*, and even the *Reader's Digest*, about the illiteracy of college applicants (Ohmann 1976).

By that time, it must be admitted, many of these applicants were supplicants, federal student aid being less easily available than in previous years. The vast web of government programs spun by Lyndon Johnson under the rubric of the Great Society had been gradually undone in Nixon's first term. Chief of Staff and one-time UC Regent H. R. Haldeman recalls that Nixon approached his project of reducing the size of government with great caution.[36] "Government spending is a lousy issue," Haldeman recalls his boss commenting at a cabinet meeting. "People are *for* spending." To sell cuts in popular programs, Nixon insisted, you have to present them as "the only way to avoid inflation and higher taxes. You never win on the question of screwing up rich kids" (Schulman 2001, 41).

Rich kids dogged Nixon's first term, as did not-so-rich ones, including those at UC Berkeley and hundreds of other campuses, protesting his prosecution of the war in Vietnam, and particularly his authorization of the bombing of Cambodia in 1970. Nixon relied on Attorney General John Mitchell to voice his administration's views. In a particularly forthright interview, Mitchell fulminated: "Those stupid kids! . . . And the professors are just as bad, if not worse. They don't know anything, nor do these stupid bastards who are running our educational institutions!" (Stroud 1970, 32).

Richard Ohmann, surely one of the professors that John Mitchell had in mind, surveyed the vast contemporary literature of complaint about this new illiteracy, and, in 1976, published his findings in the *Chronicle of Higher Education* as "The Decline in Literacy Is a Fiction, if Not a Hoax" (1976). Ohmann compiled a list of culprits that had been identified in the press as having caused this precipitous decline in the skills of young people applying for higher education. A partial reiteration follows:

The Free Speech Movement
Drugs
Zen Buddhism
Worship of the Machine
Vietnam
Abbie Hoffman
Nonverbal Parents
Watergate
Hermann Hesse
Permissiveness
The New Primitivism
Kurt Vonnegut

Ohmann adduced evidence that the nationwide drop in SAT-verbal scores and apparent declines on other measures was due to an increase in the number of people taking the tests, that is, presenting themselves for higher education. He argued that, rather than a matter of the diminishing capacity of college-age people, "[T]he conflict over literacy is a continuing political argument about who shall be educated, and what shall be the limits of equality in America" (Ohmann 1976, 32). California's Master Plan for Higher Education was, of course, all about those limits.

That same year, UC Berkeley again entered into that political argument. The impetus this time was the report, nationally circulated, that 75 percent of the students admitted to Berkeley had failed a basic writing test. Far less widely reported was the fact that the exam in question was the College Entrance Examination Board English Achievement Test, not the university's own Subject A exam. Apparently lacking this vital piece of information, the Academic Senate charged the Committee on Educational Policy with investigating the Subject A requirement and course, considering, yet again, its value, and its appropriateness in the university.

The Committee on Educational Policy reported back to the Academic Senate the usual findings: the Subject A requirement should be retained, the course was of value, and the forty-five dollar student fee for the course should be eliminated. They lamented the course's nickname, "bonehead English" and agreed that it was remedial only in those aspects of instruction that focus on mechanics. The bulk of the course, they found, addressed the development of "coherence and thought about the subject matter" and was, thus, not remedial. They concluded that "[a]ttention to these skills at the beginning of [a student's] academic career is not only justified but imperative."[37]

At the meeting of the Academic Senate, Professor William Fretter took exception to the committee's recommendation, arguing that granting credit for a nonremedial portion of a course would, in effect "redefine Subject A as a college course, when it really is just an exam." In fact, Fretter argued, it should be made an *entrance* exam and removed from the university altogether. He also reminded the Academic Senate that special state monies would no longer be available,[38] and that the cost of the course would have to come from the general budget.[39] This was clearly an undesirable expenditure, Fretter maintained, in that tight budget year. Fretter suggested that the Committee on Educational Policy consult with the Board of Admissions and Relations with Schools about the feasibility of integrating Subject A instruction into the eleventh- and twelfth-grade curricula, with the goal of making Subject A an entrance exam.

Committee on Educational Policy member Professor Charwat expressed his skepticism about Fretter's plan regarding the integration of Subject A matter into the high school curriculum: "If 50 percent of applicants can't pass the Subject A exam," he argued, "the high schools are not doing their job. The University will just have to do it."[40] The failure rate for UC Berkeley entrants on the Subject A exam was 30 percent and not 50 percent. However, the Academic Senate seems to have held itself aloof from this fact, as they seized yet another opportunity to assert the university's high standards, and to point out that the state's secondary schools, try though they might, seemed unable to meet these standards.

The only new point was raised by Professor Volman. He asked why, if half the number of admissible students routinely fail the Subject A exam, should not the requirement be eliminated altogether? With stunning good reason, he added, "Students often have many deficiencies, so why single out reading and writing?"[41] No response to his query was reported in the minutes.

In December of 1976, the University Office of Public Information announced that, for 1977, 14.8 percent of California's high school graduates would have met the university's standards for admission, not the 12.5 percent envisioned by the Master Plan, and that the standards would need some adjustments upward.[42] The newspapers took this press release and ran with it. The following day they carried articles stressing UC's stringent standards: in the *San Francisco Chronicle*, "UC Requirements May Stiffen"; in the *Los Angeles Times*, "UC Moves to Tighten Rules." The standard tightening that the University of California undertook was as follows, according to Director of Admissions Gainsley in the December 29 *San Francisco Chronicle*: high school courses in speech, drama, and journalism must require "substantial, recurrent practice in writing expository prose compositions of some length" in order to be accepted by the University as English courses. This was not a major change; many high schools reported that they had already been making such demands on their students in speech, drama, and journalism courses. But the change enabled the University of California to assert its standards. Noted Gainsley in the *San Francisco Chronicle*: "The action was harsh, but was less stringent than the one originally contemplated by the committee, which is irked because most entering freshman cannot read well enough to pass entrance exams, much less do college level work."

In the following few years, the university was engaged in an entirely different sort of debate about standards and the limits of equality. In 1978, the Supreme Court ruled in the case of *Bakke v. Regents of the University of California*. Plaintiff Allan Bakke, a white male, claimed that he was passed over for admission in favor of less qualified nonwhite applicants. A curious split decision, it was read generally as an endorsement of affirmative action, but also as a condemnation of racial quotas. Richard Donovan (1978) holds this perspective:

> A few years ago the Supreme Court seemed to heighten its authority by unanimously denying Mr. Nixon his tapes. Now it is difficult to be unanimous about anything, and the Court seems wise [in] agreeing that Allan

Bakke should be admitted to [UC] Davis, and that affirmative action should continue . . . In its urgings and admonitions, in its lack of a single vote, the Court is consistent with the broad flow of guarded, progressive legislation and fitful social progress of the past years. *Bakke* is a captive of this flow. (94)

California's public education at all levels was made a captive of another flow that year, the deep current of disappointment in government that enabled the passage in November 1978 of Proposition 13, the first volley in California's tax revolt.[43] California, like the rest of the nation, was in a very considerable recession (Dalleck 1999). California's fortunes had receded more sharply and her economic picture was bleaker. Her recession had started early on in the decade when she suffered a 9 percent unemployment rate for two years in a row (Schrag 1998, 125). Her troubles were compounded in the mid-1970s by what has been described as "spectacular" inflation in real-estate values, when the average home price went from thirty-four thousand in 1974 to eighty-five thousand in 1978 (Schrag 1998, 133). Concomitant property tax rates put California's homeowners 50 percent over the national norm (Sears and Citrin 1982, 190). Personal income tax rose 45 percent, catapulting the state into that economist's limbo, stagflation. The passage of Proposition 13 retired the bright public image of Californians as "families raising children in new developments" and presented instead the specter of "elderly homeowners unable to pay their taxes" (Schrag 1998, 142).

Through this decade of disillusionment, California's pride in her infrastructure and vast education systems had turned increasingly to grumbles about growing traffic congestion and air pollution, expansion of airports and noise pollution, looming high-rises and increasing population density, and the skyrocketing costs of public education and increasing immigration. Proposition 13's passage exposed a sullen electorate intolerant of taxation that educated "someone else's children" (Schrag 1998, 139).

CHAPTER 9

"The Technically Qualified"

> What of the students whose primary language is other than English who have been sent to the United States because of outstanding academic achievement in their home countries? Are these students remedial because they do not have the basic language skills needed to operate in another country? How do they differ from the great wave of refugees and immigrants currently swelling postsecondary institutions?
>
> *California Postsecondary Education Commission 1983, 1.*

A SURVEY PUBLISHED BY the Office of Student Research showed that between 1970 and 1980, the UC Berkeley campus experienced a 74 percent increase in the number of immigrant and refugee students.[1] This was a national phenomenon, but New York's and California's higher education systems felt the effects most strongly. Articles in both the *New York Times* and the *Los Angeles Times* reported on the rising numbers of these students, as well as on the problems that many of them had in meeting some of the demands of college-level work (Ohmann 1976). Berkeley had, in fact, expressed its concern a few years earlier. In the summer of 1978, the Office of Admissions and Records published a report noting that the student body had recently begun to include a large number of undergraduates on immigrant visas who accounted for an increase in the Educational Opportunity Program and Affirmative Action Programs.[2]

The Committee on Subject A was concerned, as well, about this changing student population. In their 1980–81 annual report, they stressed the need "to continue discussions on the implications for Subject A of the greater number of underprepared students."[3] Kim Davis, the coordinator of Subject A, did not share this concern. He maintained that this increase in immigrant students carried no special implication for Subject A. In a 1980 letter to the Subject A Committee, he reported that the percentage of Berkeley entrants held for Subject A had remained steady since the 1950s, at 35 percent to 40 percent, down from 50 percent in the 1920s.[4] Davis's implication was that the Subject A Committee was overreacting.

Davis's percentages, while accurate as a broad overview, did not address the recent, very sharp, rise in the number of students enrolled in the Subject A Program's English as a Second Language courses. ESL instruction had begun at UC Berkeley on a small scale in the 1950s, and in the early 1970s, the ESL office was repurposed to offer pre-Subject-A-level instruction, as well as a course in Subject A for ESL students. The program was named Subject A for Non-native Speakers of English. It was a division of the Subject A Program, though it was administered and staffed by ESL specialists. UC Berkeley entrants tested into the SANSE program via the Subject A exam, and were placed either into one of two pre-Subject-A-level courses, or into Subject A for Non-native Speakers. It was the SANSE program that felt most keenly the implications of the increasing numbers of underprepared students. In 1970–71, there were 242 students enrolled in ESL courses; in 1975–76, that number had risen but slightly, to 259. However, by 1980–81, the number of students in ESL courses had doubled, to 525. A great many of these students were of Asian ancestry.[5]

A report published by the Asian American Studies Program the following year noted that some 20 percent of UC Berkeley's total undergraduate population was of Asian ancestry, and some 47 percent of this group of students was foreign born. Most of these students, the report continued, had had less than 5 years of residence in the U.S. Not surprisingly, many of them presented low SAT-verbal scores. For example, of Chinese-born students, 40 percent (1343) scored under 400; of Korean-born students, 65 percent (242) scored under 400; and of Vietnamese-born students, 69 percent (78) scored under 400.[6] In the early 1980s, UC Berkeley entrants—including American-born students of Asian ancestry—presented SAT-verbal scores of 540 on average.[7] The report by the Asian American Studies Program went on to suggest that these students' underpreparedness in English skills was offset by their "spectacularly high math SAT scores."[8]

The faculty were not consoled. They reported, in a 1980–81 survey, that "their teaching had gotten harder, and that a professor can now no longer assume a common level of knowledge or skill in a classroom." Faculty were particularly concerned, the survey revealed, that "they were being asked to handle problems, especially in writing, that they were never trained to handle."[9] The *Chronicle of Higher Education* echoed these concerns in an article in its June 1, 1981 edition about the general proliferation of remedial coursework at the postsecondary level, and the *Sacramento Bee* (November 22, 1982) complained about the cost to the taxpayer of "The Bonehead Problem at the University of California."

California herself was looking at problems that economists had never been trained to handle. Nationwide, 1977–79 had been years of rapid economic expansion, accompanied by massive inflation. "Stagflation" gave way to "downsizing" in the new decade.[10] The economic malaise that afflicted the nation was especially virulent and long lasting in California. She entered 1980 with double-digit inflation. During this "deindustrialization of California" (Schrag 1998, 52) there were significant plant closures by GM, Ford, Goodyear, and Firestone, as well as the drastic downsizing and ultimate collapse of that World War II hero, U.S. Steel.

Additionally, California's economic workhorse, her defense and aerospace industries, saw large cutbacks, as her "long sweet summer of postwar prosperity" (Schulmann 2001, 139) gave way to a chilly autumn of lowered expectations. Her basic infrastructure had begun to decline in the mid-1970s, even before Proposition 13, and this slide deepened in the 1980s. By the mid-1980s, too, Proposition 13's "other shoe" had dropped, as the gap between her wealthiest and her poorest began to widen. Proposition 4 hastened this divide. This was a spending-limits initiative authored by Paul Gann and billed as intended "in the Spirit of 13" (Schulmann 2001, 211). It had passed easily in 1979, and that contributed to the "haves" and "have-nots" scenario that marked California so distinctly in the new decade.

In terms of support for public education, the University of California was among the "haves." Governor Jerry Brown was not as good a friend to the university as his father, Governor Pat Brown, had been,[11] but he did stand up for the university in 1980 in his strong opposition to Proposition 9. This was Senator Howard Jarvis's initiative to reduce personal income taxes and to exempt businesses from certain categories of taxation (Sears and Citrin 1982). Proposition 9 represented a threat to all of California's public education, certainly, but was seen as singularly inimical to the well-being of the University of California. UC President David Saxon was reported to have been "particularly outspoken in forecasting dire consequences for the University" (Sears and Citrin 1982, 144). President Saxon warned that the passage of Proposition 9 would necessitate the imposition of tuition on California residents for the first time in the university's history.

This was certainly not the first time in its history that the university had faced the dire consequences imposed by shrinking revenues and ballooning student needs. Confronted with the threat of severe budget cuts, President Saxon found himself in a quandary familiar to several of his forebears in the office. He was bound by the ethos (and, in California since 1960, the law) of mass access—the 12.5 percent solution. He was also bound by the market pressure of an enrollment-driven budget to provide coursework appropriate for all the students the university accepts. And, finally, he was bound to assert and maintain the standards expected of the jewel in the crown of California's higher education. UC Berkeley's Martin Trow framed the question so: "What will the increased costs of remedial education do to the public research university? What are the costs of not doing it?" (1984, 15). As had his predecessors, Saxon answered—or at least held at bay—the question by commissioning a study of the "extent and nature" of these remedial courses, "their costs," and the "possibility of reducing the need for them."[12]

Saxon's Committee to Study the Status of Remedial Education at the University of California had barely worked its way through the preliminaries when the legislature spoke. The 1981–82 Budget Act requested that the regents adopt the policy of insisting that students fulfill the Subject A requirement by the end of their first year of attendance in order to continue at the university.[13] The University-wide Subject A Committee voiced some concerns about this new mandate, specifically that it prevented the university from accommodating "the handful of students . . . who fail the Subject A course in spite of conscientious efforts," and that these students "tend to be EOP students who came to the University at a great disadvantage and may need extra time to catch up." Given that time, the committee concluded, "they may turn out to be creditable university students."[14] The Academic Senate was apparently in no mood to make allowances for these students beyond their first year of enrollment, however, and the policy of dismissing underprepared students after their first year was codified as Academic Senate Resolution 633(D).

SR 633(D) was an assertion of standards in a minor key. It had that split-decision timbre of *Bakke v. Regents of the University of California*. The taxpayer was assured that the university distributed its instructional resources justly, but prudently, giving questionable outsiders a year—*but no more than that*—to catch up and become a credit to their university. But really, SR 633(D) was neither a genuine educational reform nor a belt tightening in response to difficult economic conditions; very few students were dismissed after a year's failure to catch up. It was more accurately a reaffirmation of the values of the university's earliest days, when questionable students were "conditioned." Conditioned students, it will be recalled, did work for the youthful university. By their conditioned status they asserted the university's standards. They publicly defined the academic level to which the university, though public, would not sink.

Complaints about diminished standards are never more strident than in years of diminished economic health, and throughout the mid-1980s, the University of California, and particularly its flagship, UC Berkeley, embarked upon a particularly public struggle to navigate the crosscurrents of demands for access and demands for stature. Remediation, as always, was the trope that clothed the disdainful embrace.

In October 1981, William Fretter, long a proponent of removing Subject A from the university altogether, and by that time Academic Vice President Fretter, wrote to all chancellors to remind them that "the decline in basic academic skills among California's high school students is a serious and costly problem." Fretter, like many of his predecessors in University of California administrations—and in the administrations of other American universities—saw the situation as a unique and transitory one: "[O]ur present efforts to offer remedial education to students who qualify for the University but who need help when they enroll should continue only on a short-term basis."[15] Fretter, like many before him—and after him—was convinced that the solution to the University's problem with its underprepared students lay with the high schools. Despite this widely subscribed-to perception that California's high schools were failing their UC-bound students, it was not until 1982 that the regents voted to require four years of English for University of California applicants. This would seem a surprisingly dilatory action, given the decades of dismay about the declining English skills of entrants. But it would seem wholly explicable by the rules of the rhetoric of remediation.

Also in October of 1981, the University-wide Committee on Educational Policy recommended against granting academic credit for remedial work.[16] This was not a new policy, but rather a reaffirmation of the policy that the university first articulated in June of 1972. Committee Chair Harold Toliver characterized this reassertion of standards as "one small step forward" in the "current efforts to [address] the problems of remedial education and to reduce the demands on us in the future."[17] This reaffirmation of the no-credit policy, then, was "in the spirit of SR 633(D)," the one-year limit on Subject A instruction. It was codified in May of 1982 as SR 761, which denied baccalaureate credit for remedial work, including Subject A.[18] Importantly, SR 761 exempted coursework designed for students whose first language was not English.

The Language Acquisition Task Force, part of the study of remediation called for by President Saxon, endorsed this exemption for students who were nonnative speakers of English, and for whom the coursework was clearly not remedial. The task force underscored the university's role as a public university, noting that, at UC Berkeley, the number of students of Asian ancestry was rising, even as the economic status of those groups was declining. The report noted that Chinese-heritage students comprised the largest group in the Educational Opportunity Program—one-third of the total in 1981.[19]

That report was one of a spate of reports issued in the early 1980s on the extent and costs of remediation. Another was Martin Trow's (1983) "Underprepared Students at Public Research Universities." Trow confirmed that the exam scores of University of California entrants had dropped appreciably in recent years: SAT-verbal scores were down 43 points from 1972–79; College Entrance Examination Board English Composition Test scores were down 51 points from 1968–79 (24). Recent declines notwithstanding, Trow challenged policy makers to take the long view, acknowledging that the University of California's situation was neither unique nor transitory. Noting that "American colleges and universities are no strangers to underprepared students or remedial instruction," he argued that "our problems, and indeed many of our responses, are remarkably similar to those of the 19th century colleges" (19).[20] Trow saw that the reluctance to grant academic credit for remedial work comes from the faculty's "sense of the vulnerability of standards for college-level work"(21).

Promises to Keep: Remedial Education in California's Public Colleges and Universities (California Postsecondary Education Commission 1983) prodded that vulnerability by noting that, "[O]f the new freshmen admitted [to the University of California] System-wide in 1979–80, some 55.8 percent had to enroll in Subject A or equivalent courses." This large percentage prompted the authors of the report to ask "whether a course taken by a majority of students should be called remedial, or instead the entry-level English course" (33).

Promises to Keep was cited heavily in a publication released in January 1984 by the Office of the President, "Report on the Status of Remedial Instruction in the University of California." The president's report adduced many of the findings reported in *Promises*, particularly those about the widespread need for remediation among California's students in all three segments of higher education. What the president's report did not address was *Promises'* central question: if a course is deemed necessary to a majority of the students that the university accepts as qualified entrants, how can it be categorized as "remedial"? Instead, the president's report focused on who these "remedial students" were: "The University's student population has changed with the admission of greater proportions of low-income, minority, and immigrant students, who are more likely than others to have come from schools with marginal college preparation programs, or to have limited fluency in spoken and written English."

The president's report then inserted these students into a special subniche of acceptability: "Although the majority of these students are *technically qualified*, they are likely to have a greater need for remedial courses and services . . ." (emphasis added). The university had a duty to the state to admit these technically qualified students, the report averred: "All population projections indicate that minorities are a rapidly growing proportion of California's population, and this trend makes the effort to increase their representation in higher education especially critical."[21] As a public university, the University of California could do no less than embrace these students.

But it could do no more. It could not, for example, choose to identify the coursework tailored for these students as "entry-level" or "introductory," rather than "remedial," and to grant it academic credit. Although the "technically qualified" accounted for some 55.8 percent of the entering class,[22] they could be seen as none other than outliers, or exceptions to the university's normally high standards. The remaining 44.2 percent of entrants —the "truly qualified," presumably—were the ones who fit comfortably inside the University's standards; their coursework was credit-worthy.

The institutional solution in 1984, then, was not so different from that of 1884, when the University of California had the top drawer and the middle drawer. Both groups had to be accommodated at the university, but the middle drawer's disappointing attainments were to be commented upon, were to be used to assert the university's standards. In 1884, the university practiced "vigilance" in overseeing the efforts of the state's few high schools to prepare students for university-level work, and sighed that it had sometimes to accept "the unfortunate, the lazy, and the feeble-minded."[23] In 1984, the university underscored the importance of partnerships with secondary schools to increase the level of students' preparation, and sighed that "until these efforts are successful, the University must continue to provide remedial instruction for inadequately prepared minority students."[24]

CHAPTER 10

"Bonehead English"

Clearly something must be wrong with our definition of remedial work, or with our assessment of these [Berkeley] students.

D. Bartholomae, Ad Hoc Committee to Review Subject A and SANSE, Report ("Faulhaber Report"), 1989, 3. UC Berkeley Library Archives.

IN JUNE OF 1989, on the Berkeley campus, yet another task force was assembled to review Subject A. It was chaired by Professor Charles Faulhaber, of the Spanish and Portuguese Department. Predictably, the task force was charged with considering whether Subject A and SANSE were "optimally conceived . . . to bring students up to the level of competence [necessary for] entering the freshman composition sequence."[1] The committee was also asked whether either Subject A or SANSE instruction could be outsourced to a community college or to University Extension.

Unlike its predecessors, the 1989 committee was asked to address matters of racial justice. Their broad portfolio included the charge of gauging whether the Subject A and SANSE faculty and administrations were "adequately addressing the particular needs of the minority students enrolled," of considering whether the faculty members were "well chosen and supervised," and of determining whether Affirmative Action hiring procedures were being observed.[2]

The sequence of events that precipitated this review of Subject A had begun unfolding five years earlier, in 1984. That year, according to the Office of Student Research, UC Berkeley accepted 4171 freshmen, one-fourth of them of Asian ancestry.[3] To its swift and considerable regret, the administration redirected all nonblack Educational Opportunity Program applicants to other University of California campuses. Some 90 percent of these redirected students were of Asian ancestry. This decision, not surprisingly, generated great controversy and ill will, particularly among the Bay Area's large Asian-ancestry population.[4] It also generated a legislative hearing. An Asian American Task Force on University Admissions was formed, as well as a community-based Chancellor's Advisory Committee on Asian American Affairs, whose membership included two prominent Asian American jurists.

The ill-conceived admissions decision of 1984 and the attendant controversy in the press and on the Berkeley campus resulted—quite reasonably—in an atmosphere of heightened awareness of attitudes toward Asian-ancestry students. In a poll taken that year, many Asian-ancestry students reported that attitudes toward them ranged from "open hostility to subtle racism to ethnic and cultural insensitivity."[5] In the mid-1980s, half of UC Berkeley's undergraduate Asian-ancestry population was foreign born, and a very great proportion of them had taken the course in Subject A or coursework in the SANSE program. In 1988, a student member of the Committee on Undergraduate Preparation and Remediation wrote to her committee chair urging him to investigate allegations of racism in the Subject A and SANSE programs. The allegations were serious, and, while they would have been taken very seriously in any case, the climate of heightened awareness toward racism conferred upon the allegations additional gravity. In the preamble to its lengthy final report, colloquially known as the Faulhaber Report, the committee averred that "a single complaint lodged—or a perception of insensitivity expressed—by a student is *ipso facto* sufficient cause for concern."[6] In this way the 1989 task force on Subject A took on a more far-reaching mandate than had been carried by all the ancestor committees to examine the efficacy of Subject A.

The committee executed a meticulous review, peering more deeply into the workings of Subject A (and SANSE) than any other committee had done. The administrators of both programs were said to "vigorously object to what they regard as inaccurate perceptions" of their programs and they complied readily with the committee's requests for information, as well as with those of the two outside reviewers who had been brought to Berkeley to assess the efficacy of Subject A (Professor David Bartholomae of the University of Pittsburgh) and SANSE (Professor Nancy Duke Lay of the City College of New York).[7]

After an extensive review, the committee found no evidence to support the claim that Subject A and SANSE faculty or administrators were guilty of discriminatory or prejudicial behavior toward students from particular racial or ethnic groups. The committee also found no evidence of "*systematic* or *willful* problems of racial insensitivity," as had been alleged (emphasis added). The administrators and faculty of both offices, although bruised by the allegations, felt that their offices' reputations had been cleared.

Random or accidental problems of racial insensitivity, the committee argued, were another matter. They noted that "unfortunate incidents of racial and ethnic insensitivity [had] occurred in both programs." The evidence was "slight and anecdotal," consisting of "a few scattered negative comments in the hundreds of students' course evaluations,"[8] and yet cause for concern, the committee believed. The Subject A and SANSE administrators were directed to establish certain reparative procedures, to commence sensitivity training sessions for faculty, and to redouble efforts to recruit minority faculty. By the time the Ad Hoc Committee's report was issued formally in September 1989, the Subject A and SANSE offices had already begun ethnic sensitivity training sessions for faculty.

About that same time, UC Berkeley Chancellor Ira Michael Heyman acted to clear the campus's reputation as a whole for similar insensitivity toward students of Asian ancestry. It will be remembered that, even before the Subject A / SANSE controversy arose, the Berkeley campus had been under a cloud of suspicion of racism toward Asian-ancestry students. In April of 1989, Heyman held a press conference at which he apologized for the campus's "insensitive admissions policies in 1984," when low-income Asian-ancestry applicants were sent to other campuses.[9] He noted further that Berkeley's response to the report of the Asian American Task Force on University Admissions, submitted in 1985, had been to develop "new procedures and policies that would ensure fairness and provide reassurance to the Asian community" (April 6, 1989).

The Ad Hoc Committee to Review Subject A and SANSE had more on its mind, however, than reassuring the Asian community. The committee commended Subject A and SANSE administrators and faculty for "an outstanding job," characterizing them as "highly qualified, well trained, conscientious and committed to their students." Further, the report remarked pointedly that this success had been achieved "despite a chronic state of demoralization brought on by budgetary constraints, overwork, part-time employment status, political pressure, and less than cordial relations with the Administration and some other units and groups."[10]

In response to its charge that it consider the efficacy of the course, the committee conceded that instruction did seem "stale," but, importantly, they attributed this staleness to Subject A / SANSE's isolation from the rest of the academic community. How could Subject A faculty be expected "to understand and reflect the ways writing is used and valued across the curriculum" if there are no mechanisms for "productive exchange" between them and the academic departments?[11] To this end, the committee recommended that faculty members from reading and composition programs across campus participate in exchanges through which they occasionally teach in Subject A or SANSE, and that they take part in the training on grading procedures that Subject A and SANSE faculty undergo. These grading procedures and training activities, the committee found, "might well serve as examples to encourage greater consistency in faculty training and grading standards among all reading and composition courses on campus."[12]

This recommendation that the Subject A and SANSE programs be more fully brought into the academic community of the campus was a response to another of the committee's charges. It was a definitive "no" to the question of whether Subject A or SANSE instruction should be outsourced to a community college.

Another example of the Ad Hoc Committee's tentacular application of its mandate is its use of the review of Subject A and SANSE as an opportunity to respond to the question posed by President Saxon in 1980 about how to reduce the need for remedial courses like Subject A. The committee challenged the Berkeley campus to reconsider the premise of

Saxon's question—that Subject A was indeed a remedial course. To this end, the committee report included the comments of outside reviewer Bartholomae: "On the basis of both percentages [one-third of students 'held' for Subject A on the Berkeley campus] and on the quality of the students' writing, I would say that Berkeley demands more of its students for entry into the 'mainstream' curriculum than other universities."[13] In its effort to delegitimize the characterization of Subject A instruction at Berkeley as "remedial," the committee relied further on Bartholomae:

> No one seems to have meditated seriously upon the fact that anywhere from one-third (recently) to one-half (historically) of all students admitted to Berkeley in any given year are held for Subject A, and that this situation has lasted for over 65 years.[14] Most of these students are otherwise completely qualified to attend Berkeley. They have completed the basic a–f requirements and have placed among the top 12.5 percent of graduating students in the state of California. To state that these students are ready for university work in all aspects but one is very puzzling indeed. Clearly something must be wrong with our definition of remedial work, or with our assessment of these students.[15]

Next to this, the committee posed a definition of the Subject A course that clearly—surgically, even—removed Subject A from the realm of the remedial: the purpose of the Subject A course was to "introduce students to the language and methods of the University."[16]

The Ad Hoc committee recommended the merger of the SANSE and Subject A programs in a common location,[17] and suggested that the new, combined unit be called the "College Writing Programs" so as to eliminate any pejorative "Subject A" or "bonehead English" connotations.[18] The title *College Writing* packed an additional punch: it heavily underscored the nonremedial, or college-level, nature of the instruction offered. Further, pressed the committee, because instruction in Subject A is not remedial, but rather an introduction to the language and methods of the university, the course should carry full credit.

The committee recommended additionally that the new College Writing Programs be directed by a ladder-rank faculty member "with research and instructional interests in the teaching of writing."[19] It was recommended that such a faculty member be loaned from an academic department for a period three to five years, and then replaced with another professor with research and instructional interests in writing. The director's status as an Academic Senate member, the recommendation argued, would diminish the faculty's isolation, and help bring them into the mainstream of the academy, and of composition theory. This new director was to be charged with reviewing the curricula of both the Subject A course and the SANSE sequence, "with a particular eye to eliminating stale routine."[20] This charge included "instituting, extending, and monitoring the organizational, pedagogical, and personnel changes" that the report suggested.[21] Despite objections from some members of the Committee on Preparatory and Remedial Education about the feasibility of two of the Ad Hoc Committee's recommendations—the awarding of full credit for Subject A instruction, and the administrative stability of a plan with academic coordinators reporting to a director on loan from an academic department[22]—they were implemented three years later.

The College Writing Programs office was established in fall of 1992, under the aegis of Donald McQuade, newly appointed dean of Undergraduate and Interdisciplinary Studies in the College of Letters and Science. It combined both the Subject A program and SANSE. Among the "organizational, pedagogical, and personnel changes" were the elimination of the position of academic coordinator of Subject A; elimination of the SANSE sequence, as well as that program's academic coordinator position; appointment of a ladder-rank faculty member as the programs' director for a three-year term; and creation of a six-unit intensive course that combined the instruction offered in the old Subject A course with instruction at the level of the first course in the reading and composition requirement.

The design of this new course and writing program had begun in 1991 or earlier, guided in large part by Glynda Hull, professor of education and then-member of the Committee on Undergraduate Preparation and Remediation; Arthur Quinn, professor of rhetoric and founding director of the College Writing Programs; and Donald McQuade, professor of English and then-chair of the Reading and Composition Committee. Hull's portfolio included expertise as a composition specialist, as well as a highly articulated research interest in remediation as social construct. She was ideally suited to reconceive the student "held" for Subject A. Quinn's considerable knowledge of the student writer at Berkeley, his clear respect for the Subject A and SANSE faculty, and his formidable skills as a rhetorician suited him ideally for the task of navigating the course's and the program's early, difficult days. McQuade had come to composition some twenty years earlier, in the early 1970s, when he, along with colleagues Mina Shaughnessy, Kenneth Bruffee, and others, struggled to understand the issues presented by students who were filling the English classrooms of the City University of New York during those years of open admissions. From that struggle was born the construct "Basic Writer," one of the pillars upon which composition studies is built. As dean, McQuade was in a perfect position—philosophically and pedagogically, as well as administratively—to establish the College Writing Programs.

Hull, Quinn, and McQuade were determined that the new course should be both *perceived* and *conceived* as nonremedial. It was important that it be perceived as nonremedial so that it would not be vulnerable to the "Gardner Initiative," the dictum issued in 1990 by UC President David Gardner that all remedial courses be discontinued. It was important, as well, in the conception of the course, that it be crafted as more than propaedeutic to participation in the discursive communities of the academy—not as a prep class, but rather as structured immersion in those discourses. From these two concerns they dictated an elegant solution to an institutional problem and a pedagogical one. Combining Subject A-level writing instruction with 1A-level composing work, the new course gracefully sidestepped President Gardner's dictum by melding putatively "remedial" elements of instruction with work widely accepted as "entry-level" postsecondary writing. At the same time, the course was designed to bring writing at UC Berkeley more solidly into the current of thought about composition theory and practice.

Hull had earlier presented the goals of the new course to Subject A Supervisor Kim Davis. In 1991, Davis asked veteran Subject A lecturers Steve Tollefson and Gail Offen-Brown to collaborate with Hull in crafting a syllabus that addressed those goals.[23] The cover memo accompanying the course proposal relied upon the recommendations of the Ad Hoc Committee to confer legitimacy upon the proposed course, and, most particularly, upon its intended institutional home, the College Writing Programs:

> [This course] responds further and more significantly to the Committee's concern that, "despite its well established instructional accomplishments," Subject A has remained a "marginalized" program. The reasons for Subject

A's tenuous hold on academic legitimacy are of course rooted in the long history of the University's handling of "remedial" instruction. It was the Review Committee's clear intent, however, to create a situation in which Subject A and SANSE can be re-envisioned as the basic theoretical and pedagogical foundation of the campus's comprehensive—and widely distributed—writing programs.[24]

The course was approved by the Committee on Courses, and it was authorized to carry six units of credit. The College Writing Programs was established under the aegis of the Division of Undergraduate and Interdisciplinary Studies. Supervisor Davis became Lecturer Davis, and Arthur Quinn took a partial leave from the Department of Rhetoric to become director. Two new lecturers were hired, one of them an Asian American with a PhD in rhetoric and composition, the other a specialist in second-language writing with a PhD in applied linguistics.

By this lively institutional and pedagogical two-step, the Hull-Quinn-McQuade troupe slew the remedial dragon at Berkeley. But UC Berkeley wasn't quite ready to dance on his grave.

Beyond question, the new College Writing Programs' six-unit course effectively dissolved the distinction between Subject A instruction and 1A Reading and Composition instruction, between the remedial student and the regular student. But the College Writing Programs was a far cry from becoming "the basic theoretical and pedagogical foundation of the campus's comprehensive . . . writing programs" for which the Ad Hoc Committee had lobbied so tirelessly. The remedial student having been deconstructed, the remedial stigma devolved onto the agent of that change, the College Writing Programs. The Programs' recent history will illustrate this.

CHAPTER 11

"Below Acceptable Levels"

Too many students enter UC, move through the curriculum, and graduate with writing skills that fall below acceptable levels.

Office of the President, Review of the Board of Admissions and Relations with Schools, University Committee on Educational Policy, and University Committee on Preparatory Education Reports on the Subject A Requirement, September 30, 2002. UC Berkeley Library Archives.

IN 1995, HULL SUCCEEDED Arthur Quinn as College Writing Programs director, and immediately began her considerable efforts to move composition instruction in from the periphery of the academy. During her four years as director, she guided a succession of proposals for upper-division writing courses through a chilly and occasionally hostile course-approval procedure. Course approval is, and should be, a rigorous process of examination both of the course content and of the sponsoring unit's capacity to offer appropriate instruction. Course approval for these particular upper-division writing courses, however, entailed invoking the rhetoric of remediation; questions were raised as to the capacity of "Subject A staff" to teach advanced students, as well as to the College Writing Programs' capacity to enter into the mainstream of course offerings at UC Berkeley. The campus might have done away with the construct of the conditioned *student*, but it clung to the concept of "conditioning." This time, it was the *instructors* who were facing conditioning, rather than the students.

Hull and the College Writing faculty persisted, however, and, with solid support from the Division of Undergraduate and Interdisciplinary Studies, they prevailed. Four upper-division courses eventually gained Academic Senate approval. A graduate-level training course for graduate assistant instructors was approved, and it quickly expanded to welcome graduate students hired to teach reading and composition courses in various departments. Additionally, the programs developed a course to train graduate student instructors to work with student writers whose first language is not English. These were very considerable accomplishments.

Two years into her tenancy in the director's office, Hull made a strenuous attempt to enhance the College Writing Programs' status and to broaden its portfolio. In 1997, she chaired the UC Berkeley Task Force on Upper Division Writing. This task force carried the robust recommendations of the Ad Hoc Committee even further. The 1997 report insisted:

> The College Writing Programs should be at the center of writing instruction on the Berkeley campus, offering an institutional home and a driving force for various writing-improvement initiatives, such as providing the training in pedagogy for all GSIs assigned to teach composition courses, establishing an award for distinction in writing among undergraduates, and chartering a writing minor.[1]

The fate of these three initiatives is instructive in the story of the devolution of the remedial role onto the College Writing Programs: today, twelve years later, the College Writing Programs does indeed provide training in pedagogy for a large number of the campus's graduate student instructors hired to teach composition. The creative writing minor has been established under the aegis of the Division of Undergraduate and Interdisciplinary Studies. However, the upper-division courses of the College Writing Programs are notably absent from the list of courses judged worthy of credit toward the minor. The coordinator of the writing minor does entertain petitions from individual students to have a College Writing Programs course count toward the minor, but each such request entails something of a miniature course-approval process. The coordinator of the minor evaluates the course materials used that semester and the suitability of the instructor who taught the course. The College Writing Programs' course, and the instructor are, in a word, conditioned.

In terms of the goal of moving the College Writing Programs to the center of writing instruction at Berkeley, the most important recommendation of the 1997 task force was its vision of the College Writing Programs as facilitating the development of a range of discipline-specific upper-division writing courses. With regard to the importance of such specialized upper-division writing courses, Hull's committee, like the committees before hers, pressed the point that *all* writing is developmental:

> Our review of recent theory and best practices in composition makes clear [that] writing skills develop over time; they atrophy without use; and a lower-division writing sequence can't bear the entire burden of teaching the specialized conventions associated with different genres, professions, and disciplines.[2]

In its recommendations that writing instruction be recursive across a student's academic career, and that it be discipline based, this 1997 task force on writing improvement echoed the words of the Prose Improvement Committee in 1953. That earlier committee had called for instruction in writing to be recognized as "within [the purview of] the University at large, a well-founded, continuous, growing effort."[3]

So far, the 1997 Task Force's recommendation regarding upper-division writing in the disciplines has had as slight an impact upon the university at large as the Prose Improvement Committee's recommendation had in 1953. In 2001, however, this seemed about to change. UC Berkeley, along with its sisters in the University of California system, was asked to examine not just the writing competence of students about to enter the university, but also the writing competence of those about to leave the university.

In November of 2001, Provost and Vice President of Academic Affairs Judson King called for a system-wide review of the prospects for improving undergraduate writing. In his letter, King asked the by-now wholly familiar questions about Subject A and the university's perennially problematic entrants. King wanted to know, "If the current process is not achieving our goals, what new approaches would serve us better?" Additionally, he asked for "some creative thinking to help us consider alternatives beyond the current process."[4]

The College Writing Programs' approach to Subject A-level instruction made many of King's questions less relevant to the Berkeley campus than to other University of California campuses where the remedial dragon still breathes fire. But his invitation for a study that encompasses all undergraduate writing had the potential, at least, for igniting interest in upper-division writing instruction at UC Berkeley.

In the spring of 2002, in response to King's call, the University Committees on Educational Policy and on Preparatory Education voiced the widely held perception among faculty that students' writing skills seem to decline—or lithify—as they advance toward their degrees.[5] The University Committee on Educational Policy called for a study to verify this faculty belief.[6] The preparatory education committee agreed with the educational policy committee on the importance of a study of upper-division students' writing skills, and asked for background data regarding, for example, students' prior coursework and transfer units.

The University Committee on Preparatory Education recommended that more extensive writing assignments be required in coursework beyond the reading and composition sequence. They observed that "[f]aculty need to understand that students learn to write in context—in the context of the university rather than high school, and then in the context of their disciplines," and that "[w]riting skills are not learned once and for all, but progressively, as demands intensify."[7] The University Committee on Educational Policy called for "an institutional commitment to action" toward upper-division writing improvement.[8] UC Berkeley has long proven commitment-averse with regard to writing instruction in the disciplines, and this 2002 call produced the same lack of response.

This call for institutional commitment was, of course, not the first time UC Berkeley had been urged to consider offering writing instruction in the disciplines. In 1955, Professor Evans, chair of the Subject A Committee, vented his exasperation at faculty and administrative perceptions that the Subject A requirement was somehow a magical warrant that "freshmen will, four years later, write like proper seniors."[9] Rather, this call, with its complaint that "too many students enter UC, move through the curriculum, and graduate with writing skills that fall below acceptable levels," seems destined to create a new category in need of remediation: *im*proper seniors.

Like the student held for the Subject A requirement, the improper senior occasions the assertion of standards. Each chapter in this history of the rhetoric of remediation has stood for the proposition that when economic downturns and enrollment upsurges co-occur, the university embarks upon an energetic program of asserting its standards. These strenuous assertions serve to remind California of the high quality of the education her university provides, even as the institution strains to embrace every qualified child of California who thirsts for knowledge. The rhetoric of remediation regulates the tension between the demand for access and the demand for status, the tug of democracy and the lure of elitism. This most recent expression of dismay about the underperformance of student writers may indeed mark the "promotion" of the rhetoric of remediation to the upper division.

CONCLUSION

The Disdainful Embrace

> To walk backwards is to find out how to go forward.
>
> *Mankell 2008, 228.*

So, AFTER THIS EXCURSION through UC Berkeley's long engagement in the rhetoric of remediation, I have to ask: What do I have to show for my travels? What stamps are on my passport?

As I wandered through the archives, eavesdropping on long-expired conversations, I heard so much about the Eden of Proficiency, that lush and ferny place in the university's past where students' essays did not disappoint, and where standards were not chronically about to crash. I beat the bushes, but that Eden eluded me. It was nowhere to be found in UC's past, and certainly not in its present. Student writers were disappointments, it seemed, almost as soon as the ink was dry on the charter that established the university, that bold experiment to bring books to Eldorado. Like all failed explorers, I comforted myself with the thought that other explorers—better women and men than I—had failed. The Eden of Proficiency was not to be found in other campuses' pasts either. Not at the great public universities of the Midwest: Michigan, Wisconsin, and Minnesota in the 1870s; not at the eastern fastnesses of Harvard and Penn in the 1850s; not even in the colonnaded sanctum of North Carolina in the 1830s.

Likewise, never in my exploration did I fetch up onto UC's own mystical latitude, that storied place in time where the inhabitants were periodically battered by ferocious waves—of GIs, of immigrants, of the working class, of other demographic storm fronts—and then restored to sunny normalcy as soon as the storm passed over. I found no traces of storm surges of bad writers. Neither did I find evidence of standards suddenly breached and then rebuilt manfully (or more likely, womanfully) by writing-repair crews deployed to wrestle with the disaster, those crews, after the mission was declared "accomplished," shipped out to fight a composition disaster on another campus. In fact, like explorers of other universities' pasts, I saw evidence of an enduring class of composition specialists hired semester after year after decade after century to address a routine, ongoing instructional need, rather than a strike force of first responders brought in to wrench the university back from the brink.[1]

As I walked deeper into the archives, striving to map the echoes of the rhetoric of remediation, I often heard rumors of a linguistic Lourdes at UC, a place of healing where sickly new matriculants were delivered up to be cured evermore of their afflictions as writers. My explorations showed me that faith in this miraculous site was fervently held by faculty, administrators, and the public. Shock was great when the Lourdes effect was seen periodically to have failed, when students, having been vaccinated against bad writing as freshmen, seemed to develop resistant strains of improficiency as juniors and seniors. A century's worth of academic senate committees and task forces have been assigned to investigate the peculiar phenomenon of relapse among student writers. Testimony has been given at these councils by congregants less convinced of Lourdes's existence, people who argued that instruction in writing need be "a continuous, growing effort" undertaken in all departments;[2] that, without consistent instruction through their academic years, it is folly to expect that "freshmen, four years later, will write like proper seniors";[3] that "writing skills develop over time" and are "not acquired only within the freshman sequence";[4] and that "writing skills are not learned once and for all, but progressively, as demands intensify."[5] What happened to all this testimony? It was duly entered into the record, and even endorsed in some small ways. But these voices were never strong enough to form a counter-dogma to the dominant faith in a linguistic Lourdes, a grotto where freshmen could be washed clean forever of their infirmities.

So then, at the end of the expedition, like my predecessors, I had nothing to declare, except that there was no there there.[6] No place in time when students' writing did not cause disappointment and occasion the public expression of dismay. No occasion when the rhetoric of remediation did not accomplish political work, did not focus public attention on UC Berkeley's standards, and the heroic fight to maintain them.

Was it a cynical act of manipulation—of the legislature, of the taxpayers —for the rhetoricians to make up out of whole cloth a proficient, prelapsarian population of student writers? I don't believe so. I believe that it is an unthinking gesture for the builder to reach for whatever device is at hand as he lays out the foundation, raises high the roof beam. It is not surprising that these builders—men of letters, all—would use *rhetorical* devices.

Neither is it surprising that the good and godly men who made UC, and made the state, believe in their mission, would see themselves as engaged in a quest to repair the lapse that had thrust California's golden youth out of the Eden of Proficiency. Nor that their battle for state support would cast them as UC's David against California's Goliath of legislative hostility. It was all to the good that the enactment of that quest shone a golden light on the University of California, but in the battle, it was the student writer who took the friendly fire. "They could neither read nor write," they were "lazy and feeble-minded," and they were "beautiful but dumb." The tradition of embracing and disgracing them continued as the rhetoric of remediation did its work in asserting the campus's standards and helping those captains of the state's flagship university navigate the treacherous currents where demands for access crash against insistence on elitism.

So here I sit at the end of my expedition, in Wheeler Hall, built to honor the man who pushed the university into the twentieth century, and never wanted Berkeley to have a "composition mill." I'm in my office in College Writing, the composition program (if not a mill) invented to end remediation. I've just finished reading a stack of Analytical Writing Placement Exams (née Subject A Exams), and I find myself wholly willing to categorize many of the examinees as "underprepared," and to place them in a course designed to address that underpreparedness. I don't feel that I'm "holding" them or "conditioning" them, though that is, in fact, what I'm doing. I feel that I'm doing a good, helpful thing. My job. I can't help but think that my predecessors felt the same way when they read similar sheaves of exams, and declared students "remedial." I shrink from that r-word, find it a bit of a slur. But I'm not sure that my predecessors saw themselves as anything but hard-working teachers dedicated to their students' success. Like me. The same might be said of *their* predecessors who identified their examinees as "incompetent." And maybe (maybe) even the ones who characterized their examinees as "lazy." Each of us has been trapped within our own era's paradigm for asserting standards. I can't afford to blame any of my predecessors for their word choice; any day now, an up-and-coming compositionist will take umbrage at my era's use of "underprepared." The point is that every generation of men and women who have dealt with freshman writing finds students who would benefit from additional work in composing so that they might more fully participate in the academic conversation.

This book has never been about the claim that such students do not exist, or that coursework for them should be abolished. Rather, this book is about the claim that these students, even as they were benefiting from the instruction offered them, were also conferring benefits upon their university. The identification of these students as remedial, incompetent, deficient, beautiful-but-dumb, and feebleminded helped their university assert its standards at key moments in the state's and the university's political life. "Standards" in students' writing proficiency have been a political phenomenon as much as an educational phenomenon. The call for higher standards, or more significantly the outcry that they are not high enough, has been a rhetorical move in the university's complicated 140-year-long dance with the legislature, with the taxpayer, with other colleges and universities.

Now I have to ask the difficult question: does my case study have legs? That is to ask: can UC Berkeley's story of remediation offer insights to compositionists at other universities? Or is this story an odd, isolated, exceptional instance of rhetorical legerdemain from a university that has always taken an exceptionalist view of its mission? California herself was built on the notion of exceptionalism; from her earliest days she has been a special case, a land of opportunities exceptional even in a nation full of opportunities. But in the university's duty to the state, Berkeley is not different from other public universities. A public university bears many complex responsibilities, of course, but perhaps its core duty is to mediate the competing demands for access and exclusivity. The ability to offer a disdainful embrace to so many of its entrants over the decades has helped the University of California, Berkeley, in small and not-so-small ways, with that difficult balancing act. It is not within the ambit of my case study to discover if the disdainful embrace has helped other public universities perform their own balancing acts. But I would not be surprised to learn that it has.

Mankell (2008) reminds us that "to walk backwards is to find out how to go forward" (228). Walking backward through the university's lengthy engagement in the rhetoric of remediation, I've found out that the way for me to move forward is to look long and carefully at every assertion of standards, every complaint about students' disappointing writing that I hear. Going forward, I intend to look at the political, economic, and social grounds from which the complaint arises, and remember that not only are "standards" a political phenomenon as much as an educational phenomenon, but that "remediation" is a rhetorical practice as much an instructional practice. I would encourage my colleagues in composition to do the same.

NOTES

Acknowledgments

1. Ad Hoc Committee to Review Subject A and SANSE, Report ("Faulhaber Report"), 1989, 33. UC Berkeley Library Archives.

Introduction: "To Embrace Every Child of California"

1. President Kerr to Committee on Educational Policy, 1963. UC Berkeley Library Archives.

2. Subject A was originally called "Subject 1." In its early days the university classified areas of preparation as follows: Subject 1: English; Subject 2: Mathematics; Subject 3: Natural Sciences; etc.

3. Professor H. Edwards, Chair, Committee on Relations with Schools, to Director of Admissions W. A. Spindt, June 18, 1951. UC Berkeley Library Archives. See also Director of Admissions W. A. Spindt to Liaison Committee on Subject A, May 13, 1952. UC Berkeley Library Archives.

4. Professor B. Bridgeman, Chair, Subject A Committee, to Committee on Educational Policy, 1967. UC Berkeley Library Archives.

5. In 2005, the academic senate voted to change the name of the requirement from "Subject A" to the more descriptive "Entry Level Writing" requirement. This book will use the label "Subject A" throughout, as it deals mostly with the university's history from 1869 to 2006.

6. University-wide Committee on Educational Policy, Report ("Turner-Martin Report"), July 7, 1972. UC Berkeley Library Archives. This invaluable overview of Subject A's history was prepared by Ralph Turner, then chair of the University-wide Committee on Educational Policy, and by Jay Martin, then chair of the Committee on Educational Policy, UC Irvine.

7. Report on the Committee on Composition and Rhetoric, 1892. UC Berkeley Library Archives. See also the summary of this report in Kitzhaber 1990, 44.

8. Cornelius Beach Bradley Diaries, September 1884. UC Berkeley Library Archives.

9. Minutes of the Special Committee on Subject A, February 15, 1958. UC Berkeley Library Archives.

10. The fascinating story of City College's era of open access and Mina Shaughnessy's role in that story has been told from a rich range of perspectives and with great insight. See, among others, Soliday (2002), Lu and Horner (1999), Renfro and Armour-Garb (1999), Maher (1997), Mutnick (1996), and Clark (1960).

11. Dean of Letters and Science A. S. Knight to Professor B. O'Hehir, Chair, Committee on Educational Policy-Remedial Education, September 13, 1971. UC Berkeley Library Archives.

12. Office of the President, Report on the Status of Remedial Instruction in the University of California, February 15, 1984, 33. UC Berkeley Library Archives.

13. Report to the Policy Committee on the University of California's Activities to Assist Underprepared Students, March, 1981, 24. UC Berkeley Library Archives.

14. Ad Hoc Committee to Review Subject A and SANSE, Report ("Faulhaber Report"), 1989, 3. UC Berkeley Library Archives.

1. "The Honor of the State"

Title: President H. Davis to the California Legislature, Report, 1888. UC Berkeley Library Archives. Quoted in Ferrier 1930, 378.

1. Only males enrolled that first year. Women were permitted to apply in 1870, and did so that year and every year thereafter. Female performance on the Subject A exam, nearly always stronger than male, became a matter of political importance much later. This topic will be explored in chapter 6.

2. University of California President Clark Kerr was largely responsible for creating the Master Plan for Higher Education, which established a three-tier system of access to public higher education. The state's junior colleges were required to accept all of California's high school graduates; the state colleges (later state universities), to accept the top 33.3 percent of high school graduates; and the University of California, the top 12.5 percent.

3. Minutes of the Academic Council, 1870. UC Berkeley Library Archives.

4. Minutes of the Academic Council, 1872. UC Berkeley Library Archives.

5. *Oxford English Dictionary*, 2nd ed., s.v. "hoodlum."

2. "The Unfortunate, the Lazy, and the Feeble-Minded"

Title: Berkeley Professor of Rhetoric Cornelius Beach Bradley wrote this description of the composition students with whom he worked. Cornelius Beach Bradley Diaries, September 17, 1884. UC Berkeley Library Archives.

1. The missteps of eminent botanist W. L. Jepson, once a student of Bradley, were recorded in the book. Jepson's efforts on "The Benefits I Expect to Derive from a College Education" were characterized as "inexact" and "chippy." Presumably, the young Jepson derived more benefits from his undergraduate days than he was able to articulate for Professor Bradley. Sadly, though Jack London was on campus during Bradley's time, London's freshman missteps did not make Bradley's book.

2. Cornelius Beach Bradley Diaries, January 15, 1883. UC Berkeley Library Archives.

3. Cornelius Beach Bradley Diaries, February 27, 1883. UC Berkeley Library Archives.

4. Cornelius Beach Bradley Diaries, Summer, 1883. UC Berkeley Library Archives. By this time, Subject 1 was English composition, and Subject 14 was English literature.

5. Cornelius Beach Bradley Diaries, January 15, 1884. UC Berkeley Library Archives.

6. Cornelius Beach Bradley Diaries, May 28, 1885. UC Berkeley Library Archives.

7. Cornelius Beach Bradley Diaries, July 3, 1888. UC Berkeley Library Archives. To be conditioned, it will be recalled, was to have failed the examination, and to have been accepted at the University of California with the requirement of completing further remedial work.

8. Cornelius Beach Bradley Diaries, September 17, 1884. UC Berkeley Library Archives.

9. Cornelius Beach Bradley Diaries, September 24, 1888. UC Berkeley Library Archives.

10. Exam contents and results are reported in Johnson 1934.

3. "They Can Neither Read Nor Write"

Title: From Gayley, C. M., and C. B. Bradley, 1904. *Suggestions to Teachers of English in the Secondary Schools.*

1. President Davis may have gotten the mil tax for UC, but he disappointed the regents in other regards. His two-year tenure was the shortest yet for UC.

2. Wheeler was partial to Yale and to Yale faculty. Two years into his presidency of the University of California, he commented fondly, "It seems that we resemble [Yale] in a good many things . . . I believe that our color is Yale blue, only we have added to it the gold of California's hills" (Ferrier 1930, 633).

3. Bowman 1963, 40. Unpublished manuscript, UC Berkeley Library Archives.

4. The Big Four were Leland Stanford, William Crocker, Henry Hopkins, and Colis Huntington.

5. Mowry (1951) reports that the Southern Pacific Railroad engineered U.S. Senator George C. Perkins's elections. Perkins served from 1893 to 1915.

6. Stephen Field was appointed to the federal judiciary at the urging of the Big Four (Starr 1985).

7. William Crocker, one of the Big Four, owned Pacific Gas and Electric.

8. In those days, one was "called" to a university, even a secular one like UC. Wheeler, with his immense power, did all of the calling, except for appointments in the Department of Chemistry, which prerogative he acceded to the haughty and brilliant Gilbert Lewis.

9. Bowman 1963, 40. Unpublished manuscript, UC Berkeley Library Archives.

10. Full professors at Berkeley earned $3941 per year during Wheeler's era. May (1993) characterizes this as "less than at Stanford, but more than at Wisconsin" (19). An appointment at the instructor's level was worth $1457 per year, a wage that dictated prudence for a single man and a most exacting parsimony for a family man. This latter group of wage earners doubtless composed the personnel who would have separated linguistic wheat from chaff in the composition mill. (Wheeler earned $10,000 per year.)

11. Students from the College of Mechanics and Mining were said to have objected to the large numbers of female students, so Gayley limited their attendance. Gayley did not suffer women students gladly, and, on one occasion in 1904, was said to have

stalked off the podium in the middle of a lecture, angered at the behavior of some students he characterized as "giggly girls." The incident received international coverage, one Düsseldorf paper running the headline "Die Gänschen [little girl geese] von Kalifornien" (Kurtz 1943, 66).

12. Gayley could count on President Kellogg for support for most of his proposals; he was widely acknowledged as President Kellogg's "right-hand man." Kellogg stepped down in 1899, announcing to the regents: "Gentlemen, this University has a great future and I am not the one to guide its fortunes" (Kurtz 1943, 124).

13. One historically important aspect of the development of that department was Wheeler's appointment of Josephine Peixoto, the University of California's first female professor.

14. Remarks by President Kerr: Ninety-Second Charter Day Ceremonies. UC Berkeley, March 21, 1960. UC Berkeley Library Archives.

15. UC Register, 1901–02. UC Berkeley Library Archives.

16. UC Register, 1902–03. UC Berkeley Library Archives.

17. UC Register, 1902–03. UC Berkeley Library Archives.

18. Academic Council Meeting Minutes, 1892. UC Berkeley Library Archives.

19. Academic Council Meeting Minutes, December 4, 1907. UC Berkeley Library Archives.

20. Academic Council Meeting Minutes, October 12, 1892. UC Berkeley Library Archives.

21. Academic Council Meeting Minutes, March 10, 1913. UC Berkeley Library Archives.

22. Academic Council Meeting Minutes, March 10, 1913. UC Berkeley Library Archives.

23. Academic Senate Meeting Minutes, April 24, 1916. UC Berkeley Library Archives.

24. John Randolph Haynes to Hiram Johnson, December 16, 1916 (Sitton 1992, 104).

4. "Beautiful but Dumb"

1. President R. Sproul, Charter Day Address, March 21, 1931. California State Archives, Sacramento (Stadtman 1970, 262).

2. President R. Sproul and M. Deutsch to the California Commission for the Study of Educational Problems, November 6, 1930. California State Archives, Sacramento (Douglass 2000, 143).

3. Superintendent of Schools Vierling Kersey, long an opponent of the university's control over higher education, supported this conversion (Douglass 2000).

4. Academic Senate Meeting Minutes, December 17, 1931. UC Berkeley Library Archives.

5. Course reductions and class size increases were proposed by the Committee on Educational Policy, established in 1931 by Sproul to help him make academic decisions in the economic crisis.

6. President R. Sproul and M. Deutsch to the California Commission for the Study of Educational Problems, November 6, 1930 (Douglass 2000, 145).

7. President R. Sproul, Inaugural Address, October 22, 1930. California State Archives, Sacramento (Douglass 2000, 145).

8. President R. Sproul, Inaugural Address, October 22, 1930. California State Archives, Sacramento.

9. President R. Sproul to Committee on Educational Policy, November 1933. UC Berkeley Library Archives.

10. Academic Senate Meeting Minutes, November 27, 1933. UC Berkeley Library Archives.

11. Academic Senate Meeting Minutes, November 27, 1933. UC Berkeley Library Archives.

12. Academic Senate Meeting Minutes, November 27, 1933. UC Berkeley Library Archives.

13. Academic Senate Meeting Minutes, November 27, 1933. UC Berkeley Library Archives.

14. Talbott's report doesn't indicate how students' IQs were measured.

15. Subject A Office, Report of Progress by the Committee on Subject A to the Academic Council, August, 1930 (Johnson 1941, 321).

16. University Committee Meeting Minutes, Special Committee on Subject A, 1931. UC Berkeley Library Archives.

17. University Committee Meeting Minutes, Special Committee on Subject A, 1931. UC Berkeley Library Archives. (Quoted in Johnson 1941, 325.)

18. Subject A Archives, 112 Wheeler Hall, UC Berkeley Campus. (Quoted in Johnson 1941, 330.)

19. Bulletin of the Examination in Subject A, 1935. Subject A Archives, 112 Wheeler Hall, UC Berkeley Campus.

5. "The Hordes . . . Invade the Campus"

Title: In 1943, President Sproul wrote a letter to Deans Grethen, Watkins, and Hutchinson, asking "What is the University going to do after the War? Shall we be prepared for the hordes of students which some state authorities predict will invade the campus?" (Pettitt 1966, 77).

1. Report of the State Board of Education, 1939. UC Berkeley Library Archives. (Quoted in Douglass 2000, 159.)

2. The GI Bill of Rights, officially titled the Servicemen's Readjustment Act of 1944, or PL 347, guaranteed veterans up to forty-eight months of higher education or vocational training, depending on length of service. Along with five hundred dollars per year for fees and tuition, each unmarried veteran received fifty dollars per month, and each married veteran sixty-five dollars, for living expenses. Additionally, the GI Bill provided veterans with 50 percent of the funds needed to buy a home, a business property, or a farm and stock. This mortgage assistance enabled many veterans and their families

to settle in California, spurring her development. The children of these vets contributed greatly to the expansion of higher education in the 1960s.

3. Library Committee, Annual Report, 1943. UC Berkeley Library Archives.

4. University Committee Meeting Minutes, Emergency Executive Committee, January 11, 1943. UC Berkeley Library Archives.

5. University Committee Meeting Minutes, Emergency Executive Committee, January 11, 1943. UC Berkeley Library Archives.

6. Warren's strategy paid off. In early 1946, California's unemployment rate was 11 percent, but it dropped to 9 percent in early fall when veterans started college (Douglass 2000).

7. University Committee Meeting Minutes, Board of Admissions and Relations with Schools, February 13, 1945. UC Berkeley Library Archives.

8. Subject A was not an entrance exam in 1945, but an exam to sort students who had already been accepted. It is not clear in this document when the Board of Admissions proposed to change the status of the Subject A exam from a placement to an entrance exam. University Committee Meeting Minutes, Board of Admissions and Relations with Schools, February 13, 1945. UC Berkeley Library Archives.

9. Report by R. Farnham, Chair, Admissions Committee, March 13, 1945. UC Berkeley Library Archives.

10. University Committee Meeting Minutes, Emergency Executive Committee, July 18, 1946. UC Berkeley Library Archives.

11. Professor A. Gordon to Registrar T. B. Steel, August 23, 1946. UC Berkeley Library Archives.

12. University Committee Meeting Minutes, Committee on Educational Policy, July 18, 1946. UC Berkeley Library Archives.

13. University Committee Meeting Minutes, Committee on Educational Policy, July 18, 1946. UC Berkeley Library Archives.

14. Indeed, it was only as a result of World War II that Sproul was persuaded to accept UCLA as an equal to Berkeley with a role in research and graduate training.

15. Academic Senate Meeting Minutes, February 23, 1946. UC Berkeley Library Archives.

16. Examination in Subject A, 1946–51. Subject A Archives, 112 Wheeler Hall, UC Berkeley Campus.

17. President R. Sproul to Committee on Educational Policy, April 20, 1949. UC Berkeley Library Archives.

18. A pledge of loyalty was not unique to the University of California during those times; numerous other state universities exacted such a pledge of their employees (Starr 2002).

19. In San Francisco, the Hearsts owned the *Examiner* and the *Call-Bulletin*; in Los Angeles, the *Herald-Express* and the *Herald-Examiner.*

20. Among the restored dissenters was Professor David Saxon, later UC President Saxon.

6. "The Decencies of English"

Title: This was Kerr's call for writing proficiency among UC Berkeley entrants. Chancellor Kerr to Committee on Educational Policy, 1957. UC Berkeley Library Archives.

1. Kerr refers to Dean Davis as "Sailor" throughout his 2002 memoir, *The Gold and Blue.*

2. University Committee Meeting Minutes, Committee on Educational Policy, November, 1955. UC Berkeley Library Archives.

3. University Committee Meeting Minutes, Committee on Educational Policy, March 7, 1951. UC Berkeley Library Archives.

4. University Committee Meeting Minutes, Committee on Subject A, April 20, 1951. UC Berkeley Library Archives.

5. University Committee Meeting Minutes, Liaison Committee on the Subject A Problem, June 22, 1951. UC Berkeley Library Archives.

6. University Committee Meeting Minutes, Liaison Committee on the Subject A Problem, June 22, 1951. UC Berkeley Library Archives.

7. University Committee Meeting Minutes, Liaison Committee on the Subject A Problem, June 22, 1951. UC Berkeley Library Archives.

8. University Committee Meeting Minutes, Liaison Committee on the Subject A Problem, June 22, 1951. UC Berkeley Library Archives.

9. Director of Admissions W. A. Spindt to Liaison Committee on the Subject A Problem, May 13, 1952. UC Berkeley Library Archives.

10. Associate Director of Admissions G. Bird to Committee on Educational Policy, June 28, 1951. UC Berkeley Library Archives.

11. Associate Director of Admissions G. Bird to Committee on Educational Policy, June 28, 1951. UC Berkeley Library Archives.

12. Eisenhower later characterized his appointment of Warren to chief justice as "the biggest damn fool thing I ever did" (Starr 2002, 338).

13. Professor B. Lehman, Prose Improvement Project, to Professor R. Jastrow, Chair, Committee on Educational Policy, November 19, 1953. UC Berkeley Library Archives.

14. Professor J. Miles, Prose Improvement Project, to Committee on Educational Policy, 1951. See also Professor B. Lehman, Prose Improvement Project, to Professor R. Jastrow, Chair, Committee on Educational Policy, April 10, 1953. UC Berkeley Library Archives.

15. Participating departments were Anthropology, Business, Chemistry, Economics, Education, Geology, History, Political Science, and Statistics.

16. Professor B. Lehman, Prose Improvement Project, to Professor R. Jastrow, Chair, Committee on Educational Policy, April 10, 1953. UC Berkeley Library Archives.

17. Professor B. Lehman, Prose Improvement Project, to Professor R. Jastrow, Chair, Committee on Educational Policy, November 19, 1953. UC Berkeley Library Archives.

18. Professor B. Lehman, Prose Improvement Project, to Professor R. Jastrow, Chair, Committee on Educational Policy, April 10, 1953. UC Berkeley Library Archives.

19. Professor B. Lehman, Prose Improvement Project, to Professor R. Jastrow, Chair, Committee on Educational Policy, April 10, 1953. UC Berkeley Library Archives.

20. President Sproul to Committee on Educational Policy, March 1, 1954. UC Berkeley Library Archives.

21. Committee on Educational Policy to President Sproul, May 7, 1956. UC Berkeley Library Archives.

22. Oddly—or perhaps not so oddly in these postwar years when the paramount American goal for youth was for them to be "well adjusted"—the Committee on Educational Policy also noted that these studies showed that "10 percent of subnormal readers have emotional problems" (Committee on Educational Policy to President Sproul, May 7, 1956. UC Berkeley Library Archives).

23. President Sproul to Committee on Educational Policy, March 1, 1954. UC Berkeley Library Archives.

24. Even after appointing Kerr Chancellor at Berkeley in 1952, President Sproul maintained a high degree of interest and engagement in the day-to-day affairs of the campus.

25. Professor B. Evans, Subject A Committee, to Committee on Educational Policy, April 11, 1955. UC Berkeley Library Archives.

26. Professor B. Evans, Subject A Committee, to Committee on Educational Policy, April 11, 1955. UC Berkeley Library Archives.

27. Professor Connick, Chair, Committee on Educational Policy, to Committee on Subject A, May, 1955. UC Berkeley Library Archives.

28. University Committee Meeting Minutes, Committee on Educational Policy, November, 1955. UC Berkeley Library Archives.

29. Committee on Educational Policy Report, November 1955. UC Berkeley Library Archives.

30. Professor S. Bronson, University Committee Meeting Minutes, Committee on Educational Policy, September, 1955. UC Berkeley Library Archives.

31. University Committee Meeting Minutes, Committee Summary of Minutes, Committee on Educational Policy, 1956–66. UC Berkeley Library Archives.

32. University Committee Meeting Minutes, Committee on Subject A, April 2, 1956. UC Berkeley Library Archives.

33. University Committee Meeting Minutes, Committee on Subject A, April 2, 1956. UC Berkeley Library Archives.

34. University Committee Meeting Minutes, Committee on Subject A, April 2, 1956. UC Berkeley Library Archives.

35. Professor Strong, Chair, Committee on Educational Policy, to the Committee, 1957. UC Berkeley Library Archives.

36. Chancellor Kerr to Committee on Educational Policy, 1957. UC Berkeley Library Archives.

37. University Committee Meeting Minutes, Special Committee on Objectives, Programs, and Requirements, April 2, 1957. UC Berkeley Library Archives.

38. University Committee Meeting Minutes, Special Committee on Objectives, Programs, and Requirements, April 2, 1957. UC Berkeley Library Archives.

39. The members are not identified by name in the report of this meeting.

40. Professor Strong, Chair, Committee on Educational Policy, to Kerr, May 27, 1957. UC Berkeley Library Archives. Strong refers in this letter to Academic Senate regulations 265 and 475.

41. Professor Strong, Chair, Committee on Educational Policy, to Kerr, May 27, 1957. UC Berkeley Library Archives.

42. Professor Strong, Chair, Committee on Educational Policy, to Kerr, May 27, 1957. UC Berkeley Library Archives.

43. University Committee Meeting Minutes, Special Committee on Subject A, February 15, 1958. UC Berkeley Library Archives.

44. University Committee Meeting Minutes, Special Committee on Subject A, February 15, 1958. UC Berkeley Library Archives.

45. University Committee Meeting Minutes, Special Committee on Subject A, February 15, 1958. UC Berkeley Library Archives.

46. University Committee Meeting Minutes, Special Committee on Subject A, February 15, 1958. UC Berkeley Library Archives.

7. "The Tides of the Semi-literate"

Title: The Special Committee on Subject A described entrants to Berkeley thusly in their minutes of February 15, 1953.

1. Brown ultimately came to care very deeply about UC, which he referred to as "my University" (Kerr 2002, 161).

2. State of California, Senate Investigative Committee on Education, Report, 1959. UC Berkeley Library Archives.

3. The complex political story, and backstory, of the enactment of the Master Plan is told brilliantly in Aubrey Douglass's book *The California Idea and Higher Education* (Stanford University Press, 2000). My account here is a selective and perforce reductive retelling of parts of Douglass's nuanced story.

4. Kerr (2001) calibrates mass access as 10–50 percent of the age cohort enrolled in higher education; universal access as 50–100 percent.

5. In 1963, riding high on the praise accorded the Master Plan, Kerr was invited to deliver the prestigious Godkin Lecture at Harvard. With stunning prescience, he predicted that "[I]f federal grants for research brought a major revolution, then the resultant student sense of neglect may bring a minor counterrevolution" (Kerr 2001, 265).

6. Subject A Archives, 112 Wheeler Hall, UC Berkeley campus.

7. Subject A Information Booklet, 1956. Subject A Archives, 112 Wheeler Hall, UC Berkeley campus.

8. Subject A Requirement Information Pamphlet, 1961. Subject A Archives, 112 Wheeler Hall, UC Berkeley campus.

9. Subject A Exam, 1961. Subject A Archives, 112 Wheeler Hall, UC Berkeley campus.

10. All charges against the arrested students were later dropped (Rosenfeld 2002).

11. In 1956, Adlai Stevenson, barred from speaking on campus, had to deliver his campaign speech from a car parked at that corner.

12. Historian W. J. Rorabaugh offers this perspective:

The revolt at Berkeley preceded large-scale American military intervention in Vietnam and its roots lay elsewhere. The large size of the baby boom generation, the loss of unskilled jobs, and racial conflict all played a role. But in the sixties the revolts were global. They ranged from the United States to Japan to Germany to France. In Berlin, students openly modeled their revolt on the FSM and actually translated and republished some of the FSM's mimeo'd handouts. Neither Japan nor France suffered racial trouble; nor were they involved in Vietnam. What students in all these countries faced, however, was a world created and then frozen into place in 1945. World War II had peculiarly affected the United States, Japan, Germany, and France. In these four countries, the political, economic, and social rules had been rewritten in 1945. For students born just before, during, or after the war, the projection of twenty years of stasis indefinitely into the future promised the inheritance of a sterile world without any chance to alter it. (Rorabaugh 1989, 46–47)

13. These arrests were supervised by Edwin Meese III, famous later as attorney general under President Reagan, but in 1964 acting as liaison between the Alameda County District Attorney's Office and the police.

14. The fascinating story of the free speech movement has been told well by a number of historians. I am particularly indebted to W. J. Rorabaugh's *Berkeley at War* (1989); Todd Gitlin's *The Sixties: Years of Hope, Days of Rage* (1987); R. Cohen's and R. E. Zelnik's *The Free Speech Movement: Reflections on Berkeley in the 1960s* (2002); and Seymour Martin Lipset's *Rebellion in the University* (1971).

15. No figures for mothers' political affiliation were given.

16. No figures were reported for Jewish, Buddhist, or other students.

8. "Viewed as Disgraceful by Many Scholars"

Title: Faculty perceptions of the writing of many students held for the Subject A requirement. University-wide Committee on Educational Policy, Report, May 12, 1966. UC Berkeley Library Archives.

1. President Kerr to V. Robinson, Chair, Committee on Educational Policy, August 20, 1965. UC Berkeley Library Archives.

2. President Kerr to Committee on Educational Policy, 1963. UC Berkeley Library Archives.

3. Overview of Subject A for the University-wide Committee on Educational Policy, Report, July 7, 1972. UC Berkeley Library Archives.

4. Vice President A. Taylor to University-wide Committee on Educational Policy, May 12, 1966. UC Berkeley Library Archives.

5. University-wide Committee on Educational Policy, Report, May 12, 1966. UC Berkeley Library Archives.

6. Recall that the Civil Rights Act was passed in 1964.

7. University-wide Committee on Educational Policy, Report, May 12, 1966. UC Berkeley Library Archives.

8. Professor G. Pimentel, Chair, Committee on Educational Policy, to Vice President A. Taylor, May 11, 1966. UC Berkeley Library Archives.

9. Professor S. Markowitz to Professor G. Pimentel, Chair, Committee on Educational Policy, November 15, 1966. UC Berkeley Library Archives.

10. Professor S. Markowitz to Professor G. Pimentel, Chair, Committee on Educational Policy, November 15, 1966. UC Berkeley Library Archives.

11. Professor W. Shumaker to Professor G. Pimentel, Chair, Committee on Educational Policy, December 1, 1966. UC Berkeley Library Archives. Professor Shumaker's information about McClymonds High School deserved, and deserves, notice for many reasons, but they are somewhat off the point of Markowitz's demand. McClymonds was not then, nor is it now, a "feeder school" for UC Berkeley.

12. Pimentel's reference to 50 percent is based on Markowitz's claim of a 50 percent failure rate on the Subject A exam. In fact, in the year of Markowitz's letter, the failure rate was 26.6 percent, and had been below 30 percent since 1961. Pass Rates, 1967, Subject A Archives, 112 Wheeler Hall, UC Berkeley Archives.

13. Professor G. Pimentel, Chair, Committee on Educational Policy, to Professor S. Markowitz, December 9, 1966. UC Berkeley Library Archives.

14. The 2009-era reader might think to fault Professor Pimentel for subdividing the student body, by implication, into two lexical classes: "students" and "females." I'd like us to spare him the blame, or at least to generalize it to the times; in those years, the generally acceptable subdivision of the sexes was "students" and "coeds." Professor G. Pimentel, Chair, Committee on Educational Policy, to Professor S. Markowitz, December 9, 1966. UC Berkeley Library Archives.

15. In 1955–59, the average size of the freshman class was 2890; in 1960–64, it was 3991.

16. Professor C. Dekker, Chair, Committee on Courses, to Professor B. O'Hehir, Chair, Committee on Remedial Education, January 1971. UC Berkeley Library Archives.

17. Lecturer M. Wicksman, Supervisor, Subject A, to C. Jones, Chair, Committee on Educational Policy-Remedial Education, January 23, 1970. UC Berkeley Library Archives.

18. Indeed, Wicksman was replaced as Subject A supervisor shortly thereafter.

19. Though the charges against the Subject A faculty did lie smoldering, as chapter 10 maintains.

20. Professor B. O'Hehir, Chair, Committee on Remedial Education, to C. Dekker, Chair, Committee on Courses, February 5, 1971. UC Berkeley Library Archives.

21. Lecturer K. Newman to Dean of Letters and Science A. S. Knight, May 24, 1971. UC Berkeley Library Archives.

22. Committee on Educational Policy, Report on Subject A, October 11, 1971. UC Berkeley Library Archives.

23. Professor Knight to Professor O'Hehir, Chair, Committee on Educational Policy, September 13, 1971. UC Berkeley Library Archives.

24. Professor Knight to Professor O'Hehir, Chair, Committee on Educational Policy, September 13, 1971. UC Berkeley Library Archives. The Educational Opportunity Program in 1971 enrolled a considerable number of students of Asian ancestry. This special status was revoked in 1984, with results that damaged UC Berkeley's public image. It was reinstated two years later, after legislative hearings, a special committee, and a public apology from the chancellor.

25. Professor Knight to Professor O'Hehir, Chair, Committee on Educational Policy, September 13, 1971. UC Berkeley Library Archives.

26. Academic Council Meeting Minutes, April 14, 1971. UC Berkeley Library Archives.

27. University-wide Committee on Educational Policy, Report ("Turner-Martin Report"), July 7, 1972, 16. UC Berkeley Library Archives.

28. University-wide Committee on Educational Policy, Report ("Turner-Martin Report"), July 7, 1972, 28. UC Berkeley Library Archives.

29. Just a few years earlier, in 1966, Professor Donald Freeman, of UC Santa Barbara, had complained that the "Standard Academic Prose" taught in Subject A was that which enabled "the flaccid patois of organized life in the PTA and the corporation." Professor Donald Freeman to University of California, Santa Barbara, Committee on Educational Policy, May 6, 1966. UC Berkeley Library Archives.

30. University-wide Committee on Educational Policy, Report ("Turner-Martin Report"), July 7, 1972, 32. UC Berkeley Library Archives.

31. University-wide Committee on Educational Policy, Report ("Turner-Martin Report"), July 7, 1972, 18. UC Berkeley Library Archives.

32. University-wide Committee on Educational Policy, Report ("Turner-Martin Report"), July 7, 1972, 31. UC Berkeley Library Archives.

33. University-wide Committee on Educational Policy, Report ("Turner-Martin Report"), July 7, 1972, 1. UC Berkeley Library Archives.

34. Academic Council Meeting Minutes, System-wide Subcommittee on Subject A and Other Remedial Courses, December, 1975. UC Berkeley Library Archives.

35. Survey of Compositional Instruction at UC Davis, Report, October 1, 1974. UC Berkeley Library Archives.

36. Haldeman was regent ex officio as president of the Alumni Association in 1966–67.

37. Professor Fawcett, Chair, Committee on Educational Policy, to Academic Senate, April 4, 1976. UC Berkeley Library Archives.

38. Fretter was anticipating President Saxon's mandate, issued a few months later, that "continued funding for the Subject A and other remedial courses would come from

I&R budgets, not from other sources." President Saxon to Academic Senate, July 23, 1976. UC Berkeley Library Archives.

39. Estimated cost for Subject A instruction that year was $90,000–$100,000. Subject A Archives.

40. Academic Senate Meeting Minutes, April 4, 1976. UC Berkeley Library Archives.

41. Academic Senate Meeting Minutes, April 4, 1976. UC Berkeley Library Archives.

42. Office of Public Relations, Press Release, December 2, 1976. UC Berkeley Library Archives.

43. For more on Proposition 13, see Schrag 1998.

9. "The Technically Qualified"

Title: Description made in 1984 by the Office of the UC President of many University of California entrants. Office of the President, Report on the Status of Remedial Instruction in the University of California, February 15, 1984. UC Berkeley Library Archives.

1. Office of Student Research, Survey of Immigrant and Refugee Students, October, 1980. UC Berkeley Library Archives.

2. Office of Admissions and Records, Undergraduate Foreign Student Review, July, 1978. UC Berkeley Library Archives.

3. Committee on Subject A, Annual Report, 1980–81. UC Berkeley Library Archives.

4. Professor Davis to Subject A Committee, 1980. UC Berkeley Library Archives.

5. Enrollment Statistics. Subject A Archives, 112 Wheeler Hall, UC Berkeley Campus.

6. Asian-American Studies Program, Asian-American Report 13, May, 1981. UC Berkeley Library Archives.

7. University of California, California State University, and Community College students combined presented an average SAT-verbal score of 425, one point below the national average (California Postsecondary Education Commission 1983, 2).

8. Asian-American Studies Program, Asian-American Report 13, May, 1981, 1. UC Berkeley Library Archives.

9. Report to the Policy Committee on the University of California's Activities to Assist Underprepared Students, March, 1981, 24. UC Berkeley Library Archives.

10. The words *stagflation* and *downsizing* came to us in 1979. *Stagflation* debuted in the American lexicon in the *New York Review of Books*: "Stagflation ate away at prosperity" (*OED*, 2nd ed., 1996). *Downsizing*, an American coinage, entered the lexicon as an economic term in *Newsweek*. Its previous life was as an engineering term; it was born in the auto industry during the Arab Oil Embargo of 1973 (*OED*, 2nd ed., 1996).

11. Governor Jerry Brown was said to have spent much of his administration "berating the state's schools and universities for their wastefulness," regularly threatening to withhold funding. He attended UC regents meetings sporadically, and was once said to remark at a meeting: "Never has education been so irrelevant to more kids" (Schell 1978, 153).

12. President Saxon to Academic Senate, 1980. Office of the President, Report on the Status of Remedial Instruction in the University of California, February 15, 1984. UC Berkeley Library Archives.

13. Academic Senate to University-wide Committee on Educational Policy, September 1981. UC Berkeley Library Archives.

14. Professor S. Blau, Chair, University-wide Subject A Committee, to Professor O. Johnson, Chair, Academic Council, October 1, 1981. UC Berkeley Library Archives.

15. Vice President W. Fretter to chancellors, October 16, 1981. UC Berkeley Library Archives.

16. University Committee Meeting Minutes, University-wide Committee on Educational Policy, October 8, 1981. UC Berkeley Library Archives.

17. Professor H. Toliver, Chair, University-wide Committee on Educational Policy, to Henry Alder, Board of Admissions and Relations with Schools, October 13, 1981. UC Berkeley Library Archives. Importantly, Toliver reassured Alder that the policy would not affect courses that combine remedial work with college-level work. This exemption figures substantially into UC Berkeley's solution to the "problem," and will be considered later in this chapter.

18. In spring of 1983, Asian American Studies 1, a course that satisfied the Subject A requirement, was reduced from five to two baccalaureate credits in order to be compliant with SR 761. Similar reductions in SANSE 1A were made that same quarter (R. Feingold, Chair, Committee on Courses, Report on Asian American Studies, April 26, 1984. UC Berkeley Library Archives.)

19. Report and Recommendations: Language Acquisition Task Force, October, 1982. UC Berkeley Library Archives

20. Trow is, of course, not alone in this perception. David Russell and James Berlin, among others, have made similar observations to Trow's with regard to composition instruction.

21. Office of the President, Report on the Status of Remedial Instruction in the University of California, February 15, 1984, 7–9. UC Berkeley Library Archives.

22. Based on 1979–80 enrollment figures (California Postsecondary Education Commission 1983, 33).

23. Cornelius Beach Bradley Diaries, January 15, 1884. UC Berkeley Library Archives.

24. Office of the President, Report on the Status of Remedial Instruction in the University of California, February 15, 1984, 9. UC Berkeley Library Archives.

10. "Bonehead English"

Title: The November 17, 1974 issue of Time Magazine offered the University of California, Berkeley, the dubious credit of this coinage: "Almost half the freshmen at the University of California at Berkeley flunked an English composition exam this fall. They have had to enroll in a remedial course known around the campus as 'Bonehead English.'"

1. Report on Subject A at the University of California, June 21, 1989, 1. UC Berkeley Library Archives.

2. Report on Subject A at the University of California, June 21, 1989. UC Berkeley Library Archives.

3. Office of Student Research statistics for 1989–2008 are available at http://osr.berkeley.edu.

4. Report of the Chancellor's Advisory Committee, April, 1985. UC Berkeley Library Archives.

5. Report of the Chancellor's Advisory Committee, April, 1985. UC Berkeley Library Archives.

6. Ad Hoc Committee to Review Subject A and SANSE, Report ("Faulhaber Report"), 1989. UC Berkeley Library Archives.

7. Ad Hoc Committee to Review Subject A and SANSE, Report ("Faulhaber Report"), 1989. UC Berkeley Library Archives.

8. Ad Hoc Committee to Review Subject A and SANSE, Report ("Faulhaber Report"), 1989, 24. UC Berkeley Library Archives.

9. Public Information Office, Heyman, Press Release, April 6, 1989. UC Berkeley Library Archives.

10. Ad Hoc Committee to Review Subject A and SANSE, Report ("Faulhaber Report"), 1989, 13. UC Berkeley Library Archives.

11. Ad Hoc Committee to Review Subject A and SANSE, Report ("Faulhaber Report"), 1989, 18. UC Berkeley Library Archives.

12. Ad Hoc Committee to Review Subject A and SANSE, Report ("Faulhaber Report"), 1989, 16. UC Berkeley Library Archives.

13. Professor D. Bartholomae to Ad Hoc Committee to Review Subject A and SANSE, May 17, 1989, 5. UC Berkeley Library Archives.

14. Bartholomae undercalculated the longevity of the tradition; by 1989, the practice of "holding" or "conditioning" students was a bit more than one hundred years old.

15. Ad Hoc Committee to Review Subject A and SANSE, Report ("Faulhaber Report"), 1989, 33. UC Berkeley Library Archives.

16. Ad Hoc Committee to Review Subject A and SANSE, Report ("Faulhaber Report"), 1989, 18. UC Berkeley Library Archives.

17. The Subject A offices were located in the center of campus in the Dwinelle Annex, but the SANSE offices were at some remove, on the southeastern corner of campus in a converted Victorian house near Boalt Hall.

18. Bartholomae's report characterized various of the practices and attitudes of Subject A faculty and administration as partaking inappropriately of remedial approaches and methods: "The legacy of remedial instruction . . . haunts the program" (Professor D. Bartholomae to Ad Hoc Committee to Review Subject A and SANSE, May 17, 1989, 3. UC Berkeley Library Archives). Bartholomae recommended specific curricular changes to exorcise those ghosts.

19. Ad Hoc Committee to Review Subject A and SANSE, Report ("Faulhaber Report"), 1989, 15. UC Berkeley Library Archives.

20. Ad Hoc Committee to Review Subject A and SANSE, Report ("Faulhaber Report"), 1989, 19. UC Berkeley Library Archives.

21. Ad Hoc Committee to Review Subject A and SANSE, Report ("Faulhaber Report"), 1989, 15. UC Berkeley Library Archives.

22. Professor F. Crews, Chair, Committee on Preparatory and Remedial Education, to Dean of Letters and Science C. Christ, September 1, 1989. UC Berkeley Library Archives.

23. Lecturer S. Tollefson et al., Subject A Program, to Director K. Davis, Subject A Program, March 5, 1992. UC Berkeley Library Archives.

24. Supervisor K. Davis to Committee on Courses of Instruction, April 17, 1991. UC Berkeley Library Archives.

11. "Below Acceptable Levels"

1. Task Force on Improving and Increasing Writing Instruction at the Upper Division Level, Report, October 6, 1997. UC Berkeley Library Archives.

2. Task Force on Improving and Increasing Writing Instruction at the Upper Division Level, Report, October 6, 1997. UC Berkeley Library Archives.

3. Professor B. Lehman, Prose Improvement Project, to Professor R. Jastrow, Chair, Committee on Educational Policy, November 19, 1953. UC Berkeley Library Archives.

4. Provost and Vice President of Academic Affairs J. King to Professor V. Visnawathan, Chair, Academic Planning Council, November 26, 2001. UC Berkeley Library Archives.

5. Office of the President, Review of the Board of Admissions and Relations with Schools, University Committee on Educational Policy, and University Committee on Preparatory Education Reports on the Subject A Requirement, September 30, 2002. UC Berkeley Library Archives.

6. University Committee Meeting Minutes, University-wide Committee on Educational Policy, April 12, 2002. UC Berkeley Library Archives.

7. University Committee Meeting Minutes, University-wide Committee on Preparatory Education, May 10, 2002. UC Berkeley Library Archives.

8. University Committee Meeting Minutes, University-wide Committee on Educational Policy, May 29, 2002. UC Berkeley Library Archives.

9. Professor B. Evans, Chair, Subject A Committee, to Committee on Educational Policy, April 11, 1955. UC Berkeley Library Archives.

Conclusion: The Disdainful Embrace

1. Crowley (1998) and many other compositionists see this group of teachers as an underclass. At UC Berkeley, composition specialists have for very many years borne the curious employment classification of "temporary academic staff," although the need for their professional services has been anything but temporary.

2. Professor B. Lehman, Chair, Prose Improvement Project, to Professor R. Jastrow, Chair, Committee on Educational Policy, April 10, 1953. UC Berkeley Library Archives.

3. Professor B. Evans, Chair, Subject A Committee, to Committee on Educational Policy, April 11, 1955. UC Berkeley Library Archives.

4. Task Force on Improving and Increasing Writing in the Upper Division, Report, October 6, 1997. UC Berkeley Library Archives.

5. Review of Board of Admissions and Relations with Schools, University-wide Committee on Educational Policy, University-wide Committee on Preparatory Education, Report, April 12, 2002. UC Berkeley Library Archives.

6. With gratitude to the memory of Gertrude Stein and her subject, Berkeley's nearest neighbor, Oakland, the city *down* the hill.

WORKS CITED

Archival materials are listed in a separate section of this list, and are cited in the numbered notes.

Bancroft, H. H. [188?]. *Annals of the California Gold Era: 1848–1859*. New York: Bancroft.

Barth, G. 1994. *California's Practical Period: A Cultural Context of the Emerging University, 1850s–1870s*. Berkeley: Center for Studies in Higher Education and Institution for Governmental Studies, University of California.

Beck, W. A., and D. A. Williams. 1972. *California: A History of the Golden State*. Garden City, N.Y.: Doubleday.

Berlin, J. 1987. *Rhetoric and Reality: Writing Instruction in American Colleges, 1900–1985*. Carbondale: Southern Illinois University Press.

Boddam-Whetham, J. W. 1874. *Western Wanderings: A Record of Travel in the Evening Land*. London: Richard Bentley and Son.

Brereton, J., ed. 1995. *The Origins of Composition Studies in the American College, 1875–1925: A Documentary History*. Pittsburgh: University of Pittsburgh Press.

California Postsecondary Education Commission. 1983. *Promises to Keep: Remedial Education in California's Public Colleges and Universities*. Sacramento: California Postsecondary Education Commission.

Carpenter, G. R. 1895. Review of *English in American Universities*, ed. W. M. Payne. *The Educational Review*, November. Quoted in Kurtz 1943, 122.

Clark, B. 1960. *The Open-Door College*. New York: McGraw-Hill.

Cohen, R., and R. E. Zelnick. 2002. *The Free Speech Movement: Reflections on Berkeley in the 1960s*. Berkeley: University of California Press.

Conmy, P. 1928. *History of the Entrance Requirements of the Liberal Arts Colleges of the University of California*. Berkeley: University of California Press.

Crowley, S. 1998. *Composition in the University: Historical and Polemical Essays*. Pittsburgh: University of Pittsburgh Press.

Curti, M., and V. Carstensen. 1949. *The University of Wisconsin: A History*. Madison: University of Wisconsin Press. Quoted in Douglass 2000, 83.

Dalleck, R. 1999. *Ronald Reagan and the Politics of Symbolism*. Cambridge, Mass.: Harvard University Press.

Donovan, R. 1978. Bakke and "Qualified" Undergraduates. In *Admitting and Assisting Students after Bakke*, ed. A. Astin, B. Fuller, and K. Green, 85–94. San Francisco: Jossey-Bass.

Douglas, W. 1996. Rhetoric for the Meritocracy: The Creation of Composition at Harvard. In *English in America: A Radical View of the Profession*, ed. R. Ohmann, 97–132. Hanover, N.H.: Wesleyan University Press. (Orig. pub. 1976.)

Douglass, J. A. 2000. *The California Idea and American Higher Education: 1850 to the Master Plan*. Stanford: Stanford University Press.

Duff, S. E. 1945. Correlation of the University of California Subject A Exams. PhD diss., University of California, Berkeley.

Ferrier, W. W. 1930. *The Origin and Development of the University of California*. Berkeley: Sather Gate Books.

Fisher, W. M. 1876. *The Californians*. London: Macmillan. Quoted in Starr 1981, 129.

Gayley, C. M. 1895. The University of California. In *English in American Universities, by Professors in the English Departments of Twenty Representative Institutions*, ed. W. M. Payne. Boston: D. C. Heath. Reprinted in Brereton 1995, 168–72.

Gayley, C. M., and C. B. Bradley. 1894. *Suggestions to Teachers of English in the Secondary Schools*. Berkeley: University of California Press.

———. 1904. *Suggestions to Teachers of English in the Secondary Schools*. 2nd ed. Berkeley: University of California Press.

George, H. 1871. *Our Land and Land Policy, National and State*. San Francisco: White and Bauer.

Gitlin, T. 1987. *The Sixties: Years of Hope, Days of Rage*. Toronto and New York: Bantam.

Hill, A. S. 1879. An Answer to the Cry for More English. In *Twenty Years of School and College English*. Cambridge, Mass.: Harvard University Press, 1896. Reprinted in Brereton 1995, 45–56.

Hittell, J. S. 1863. *The Resources of California*. San Francisco: A. L. Bancroft and Co. Quoted in Starr 1981, 129.

House Un-American Activities Committee. 1959. *Language as a Communist Weapon; Consultation with Dr. Stefan T. Possony. Committee on Un-American Activities, House of Representatives*, Eighty-Sixth Congress, First Session. Washington, D.C.: U.S. Government Printing Office, 1959.

Horner, B., and M. Z. Lu. 1999. *Representing the 'Other': Basic Writers and the Teaching of Basic Writing*. Urbana, Ill.: National Council of Teachers of English.

Hudson, A. P. 1938. The Perennial Problem of the Ill-Prepared. *College English* 27: 727–33.

Hull, G. 1999. Alternatives to Remedial Writing: Lessons from Theory, from History, and a Case in Point. Unpublished manuscript.

Jaehn, T. 1998. Four Eras: Changes of Ownership. In *Sunset Magazine: A Century of Western Living, 1898–1998: Historical Portraits and a Chronological Bibliography of Selected Topics*, 77–105. Stanford: Stanford University Libraries. http://sunset-magazine.stanford.edu/body_index.html (accessed June 2, 2002).

Johnson, L. 1941. *The Administrative Function of English in the University of California: Examination in Subject A*. Berkeley: University of California Press.

Johnson, M. S. 1993. *The Second Gold Rush: Oakland and the East Bay in World War II*. Berkeley: University of California Press.

Jordan, D. S. 1903. University Tendencies in America. *The Popular Science Monthly* 63 (June 1903): 143–44. Quoted in Douglass 2000, 99.

Kerr, C. 1995. *The Uses of the University*. Cambridge, Mass.: Harvard University Press. (Orig. pub. 1963.)

———. 2001. *The Gold and the Blue: A Personal Memoir of the University of California, 1949–1967*, vol. 1. Berkeley: University of California Press.

Kitzhaber, A. R. 1990. *Rhetoric in American Colleges: 1850–1900*. Dallas: Southern Methodist University Press.

Kurtz, B. F. 1943. *Charles Mills Gayley*. Berkeley: University of California Press.

Leman, N. 1999. *The Big Test*. New York: Farrar, Straus and Giroux.

Life Magazine. 1950. The Regents versus the Professors. October 2.

Lipset, S. M., and S. S. Wolin, eds. 1965. *The Berkeley Student Revolt: Factors and Interpretations*. Garden City, N.Y.: Anchor/Doubleday.

———. 1971. *Rebellion at the University*. Boston: Little, Brown and Co.

Maher, J. 1997. *Mina Shaughnessy: Her Life and Work*. Urbana, Ill.: National Council of Teachers of English.

Malone, M., and R. Etulain. 1989. *The American West: A Twentieth-Century History*. Lincoln: University of Nebraska Press.

Mankell, H. 2008. *Kennedy's Brain*. New York: Vintage.

May, H. 1993. *The Three Faces of Berkeley: Competing Ideologies in the Wheeler Era, 1899–1919*. Berkeley: Center for Studies in Higher Education and Institution for Governmental Studies, University of California.

McWilliams, C. 1970. *Factories in the Field: The Story of Migratory Labor in California*. Santa Barbara, Calif.: Peregrine Press.

Miller, C. 1979. Benny Ide. *Cornell Alumni News*, September: 12–13.

Mowry, G. 1951. *The California Progressives*. New York: Oxford University Press.

Muscatine, C. 1968. *Education at Berkeley ("The Muscatine Report")*. Berkeley: University of California Press.

Mutnick, D. 1996. *Writing in an Alien World: Basic Writing and the Struggle for Equality in Higher Education*. Portsmouth, N.H.: Boynton/Cook-Heinemann.

National Policies Commission. 1944. *Education for All American Youth*. Washington, D.C.: Educational Policies Commission, National Education Association of the United States and the American Association of School Administrators. Quoted in Douglass 2000, 191.

Ohmann, R. 1976. The Decline in Literacy Is a Fiction, if Not a Hoax. *The Chronicle of Higher Education*, November 25: 32.

———. 1996. *English in America: A Radical View of the Profession*. Hanover, N.H.: Wesleyan University Press. (Orig. pub. 1976.)

Pettitt, G. 1966. *Twenty-eight Years in the Life of a University President*. Berkeley: University of California Press.

Powers, S. 1872. *Afoot and Alone: A Walk from Sea to Sea by the Northern Route*. Hartford, Conn.: Columbian Book Company. Quoted in Starr 1996, 449.

Renfro, S., and A. Armour-Garb. 1999. *Open Admissions and Remedial Education at the City University of New York*. Report Submitted to the Mayor's Advisory Task Force on the City of New York.

Rorabaugh, W. J. 1989. *Berkeley at War*. New York: Oxford University Press.

Rose, M. 1985. The Language of Exclusion. *College English* 47 (5): 341–59.

Rosenfeld, S. 2002. Reagan, Hoover, and the UC Red Scare. *San Francisco Chronicle*, June 9, special section.

Rudolph, F. 1962. *The American College and University: A History*. New York: Knopf.

Russell, D. 1992. *Writing in the Academic Disciplines, 1870–1990: A Curricular History*. Carbondale: Southern Illinois University Press.

Schell, O. 1978. *Brown*. New York: Random House.

Schrag, P. 1998. *Paradise Lost*. New York: The New Press.

Schulman, B. 2001. *The Seventies: American Culture, Society, and Politics*. New York: DaCapo/Free Press/Simon and Schuster.

Scott, B. A. 1983. *Crisis Management in Higher Education*. New York: Praeger.

Sears, D., and J. Citrin. 1982. *The Tax Revolt: Something for Nothing in California*. Cambridge, Mass.: Harvard University Press.

Shakespeare, William. 1997. *Julius Caesar*. In *The Complete Works of Shakespeare*, ed. David Bevington, 4th ed., 1021–1059. New York: Longman.

Sheils, M. 1975. Why Johnny Can't Write. *Newsweek* 92 (December 8): 58–65.

Sinclair, U. 1923. *The Goose-Step: A Study of American Education*. Pasadena, Calif.: The Author. Reprinted in 1970, New York: AMS Press. Quoted in Douglass 2000, 144.

Sitton, T. 1992. *John Randolph Haynes: California Progressive*. Stanford: Stanford University Press. Quoted in Douglass 2000, 83.

Slosson, E. 1910. *Great American Universities*. New York: Macmillan.

Smelser, N. 1974. Growth, Structural Change, and Conflict in Public Higher Education, 1950–1970. In *Public Higher Education in California*, ed. N. Smelser and G. Almond. Berkeley: University of California Press.

Soliday, M. 2002. *Politics of Remediation: Institutional and Student Needs in Higher Education*. Pittsburgh: University of Pittsburgh Press.

Soulé, F. 1998. *Annals of San Francisco*. Berkeley: Berkeley Hills Books. (Orig. pub. 1855.)

Sproul, R. 1931. Certain Aspects of the Junior College. *Junior College Journal* (February 1931): 276–77. Quoted in Douglass 2000, 147.

Stadtman, V. 1970. *The University of California, 1868–1968*. New York: McGraw-Hill.

Starr, K. 1981. *Americans and the California Dream: 1850–1915*. Santa Barbara, Calif.: Peregrine Smith.

———. 1985. *Inventing the Dream: California through the Progressive Era*. New York: Oxford University Press.

———. 1996. *Endangered Dream: The Great Depression in California*. New York: Oxford University Press.

———. 1998. Sunset Magazine and the Phenomenon of the Far West. In *Sunset Magazine: A Century of Western Living, 1898–1998: Historical Portraits and a Chronological Bibliography of Selected Topics*, 31–75. Stanford: Stanford University Libraries. http://sunset-magazine.stanford.edu/body_index.html (accessed June 2, 2002).

———. 2002. *The Dream Endures: California in the 1950s*. New York: Oxford University Press.

Stewart, G. R. 1950. *The Year of the Oath: The Fight for Academic Freedom at the University of California*. Garden City, N.Y.: Doubleday. Quoted in Starr 2002, 314.

———. 1968. *The Department of English at the University of California at Berkeley, 1868–1940*. Berkeley: University of California Press.

Stroud, K. 1970. Attorney General's Mouth Bigger than Martha's? *Women's Wear Daily,* September 18: 32. Quoted in Schulmann 2001, 41.

Suzzallo, H. 1932. *State Higher Education in California.* New York: The Carnegie Commission for the Advancement of Teaching.

Swett, J. 1911. *Public Education in California: Its Origin and Development, with Personal Reminiscences of Half a Century.* New York: American Book Co. Quoted in Douglass 2000, 98.

Talbott. 1929. English A and High School Grades. *California Quarterly of Secondary Education* 5(4): 348–53.

Taylor, W. 1929. *A National Survey of Conditions in Freshman English.* Madison: University of Wisconsin. Excerpted in Brereton 1995, 546.

Time Magazine. 1974. Bonehead English. November 17. http://www.time.com/time/magazine/article/0,9171,911515,00.html (accessed June 29, 2009).

Trimbur, J. 1991. Literacy and the Discourse of Crisis. In *Politics of Writing Instruction: Postsecondary,* eds. R. Bullock, J. Trimbur, and C. Schuster, 277–95. Portsmouth, N. H.: Boynton/Cook.

Trow, M. 1983. Underprepared Students at Public Research Universities. In *Underprepared Learners,* ed. Patricia Cross, 16–26. Washington, D.C.: American Association of Higher Education.

———. 1984. *Carnegie Commission National Survey of Undergraduate Education.* Ann Arbor: Institute for Social Research, University of Michigan.

Veysey, L. 1965. *The Emergence of the American University.* Chicago: University of Chicago Press.

Wechsler, H. 1977. *The Qualified Student: A History of Selective College Admissions in America.* New York: John Wiley and Sons.

Wells, C. 1914. *A Book of Prose Narratives.* Boston and New York: Ginn and Co.

West, G. 1931. The Administration of Subject A at the University of California. PhD diss., University of California, Berkeley.

UC Berkeley Archival Sources Cited

Unpublished Manuscripts

Bowman, J. 1963. Reminiscences of the University of California, 1906–1912. Berkeley: University of California Archives, Bancroft Library.

Register of the University

1901–02
1902–03

Academic Council Meeting Minutes

1870 (Annual)
1872 (Annual)
October 12, 1892

December 4, 1907
March 10, 1913
April 14, 1971

Academic Senate Meeting Minutes

April 24, 1916
December 17, 1931
November 27, 1933
February 23, 1946
April 4, 1976

University Committee Meeting Minutes

Special Committee on Subject A, 1931.
Emergency Executive Committee, January 11, 1943.
Board of Admissions and Relations with Schools, February 13, 1945.
Admissions Committee, March 13, 1945.
Committee on Educational Policy, July 18, 1946.
Emergency Executive Committee, July 18, 1946.
Committee on Educational Policy, April 20, 1949.
Committee on Educational Policy, March 7, 1951.
Committee on Subject A, April 20, 1951.
Liaison Committee on the Subject A Problem, June 22, 1951.
Special Committee on Subject A, February 15, 1953.
Committee on Educational Policy, September, 1955.
Committee on Educational Policy, November, 1955.
Committee on Subject A, April 2, 1956.
Special Committee on Objectives, Programs, and Requirements, April 2, 1957.
Special Committee on Subject A, February 15, 1958.
Summary of Minutes, Committee on Educational Policy, 1956–66.
Committee on Subject A, 1967.
Committee on Educational Policy-Committee on Remedial Education, January, 1971.
Committee on Educational Policy-Committee on Remedial Education, February 5, 1971.
Overview of Subject A for the University-wide Committee on Educational Policy,
    July 7, 1972.
Survey of Compositional Instruction at UC Davis, October 1, 1974.
System-wide Subcommittee on Subject A and Other Remedial Courses, December, 1975.
University-wide Committee on Educational Policy, October 8, 1981.
University-wide Committee on Preparatory Education, May 10, 2002.
University-wide Committee on Educational Policy, May 29, 2002.

Reports

Report on the Committee on Composition and Rhetoric, 1892.
Library Committee, Annual Report, 1943.

Works Cited

Report by R. Farnham, Chair, Admissions Committee, March 13, 1945.

Committee on Educational Policy Report, November 1955.

State of California, Senate Investigative Committee on Education, Report, 1959.

University-wide Committee on Educational Policy, Report, May 12, 1966.

Committee on Educational Policy, Report on Subject A, October 11, 1971.

Overview of Subject A for the University-wide Committee on Educational Policy, Report, July 7, 1972.

University-wide Committee on Educational Policy, Report ("Turner-Martin Report"), July 7, 1972. Quoted in Hull 1999, 13.

Survey of Compositional Instruction at UC Davis, Report, October 1, 1974.

System-wide Subcommittee on Subject A and Other Remedial Courses, Report, December, 1975.

Report by C. Fawcett, Chair, Committee on Educational Policy, April 4, 1976.

Office of Admissions and Records, Undergraduate Foreign Student Review, July, 1978.

Office of Student Research, Survey of Immigrant and Refugee Students, October, 1980.

Committee on Subject A, Annual Report, 1980–81.

Report to the Policy Committee on the University of California's Activities to Assist Underprepared Students, March, 1981.

Asian-American Studies Program, Asian-American Report 13, May, 1981.

Report and Recommendations: Language Acquisition Task Force, October, 1982.

Office of the President, Report on the Status of Remedial Instruction in the University of California, February 15, 1984.

Report of the Chancellor's Advisory Committee, April, 1985.

Report on Subject A at the University of California, June 21, 1989.

Ad Hoc Committee to Review Subject A and SANSE, Report ("Faulhaber Report"), 1989.

Task Force on Improving and Increasing Writing Instruction at the Upper Division Level, Report, October 6, 1997.

Office of the President, Review of Board of Admissions and Relations with Schools, University-wide Committee on Educational Policy, University-wide Committee on Preparatory Education: Reports on the Subject A Requirement, September 30, 2002.

Press Releases

Office of Public Relations, Press Release, December 2, 1976.

Public Information Office, Heyman, Press Release, April 6, 1989.

Speeches

Kerr, C. Remarks by President Kerr: Ninety-second Charter Day Ceremonies. UC Berkeley, March 21, 1960.

Diaries, Professor Cornelius Beach Bradley

January 15, 1883

February 27, 1883

Summer, 1883
January 15, 1884
September 17, 1884
May 28, 1885
July 3, 1888
September 24, 1888

Letters

Professor J. Royce to G. B. Coale, 1878.

President R. Sproul to Committee on Educational Policy, November, 1933.

Professor A. Gordon to Registrar T. B. Steel, August 23, 1946.

President R. Sproul to Committee on Educational Policy, April 20, 1949.

Professor H. Edwards, Chair, Committee on Relations with Schools, to Director of Admissions W. A. Spindt, June 18, 1951.

Associate Director of Admissions G. Bird to Committee on Educational Policy, June 28, 1951.

Professor J. Miles, Chair, Prose Improvement Project, to Committee on Educational Policy, 1951.

Director of Admissions W. A. Spindt to Liaison Committee on the Subject A Problem, May 13, 1952.

Professor B. Lehman, Chair, Prose Improvement Project, to Professor R. Jastrow, Chair, Committee on Educational Policy, April 10, 1953.

Professor B. Lehman, Chair, Prose Improvement Project, to Professor R. Jastrow, Chair, Committee on Educational Policy, November 19, 1953.

President Sproul to Committee on Educational Policy, March 1, 1954.

Professor B. Evans, Chair, Subject A Committee, to Committee on Educational Policy, April 11, 1955.

Professor Connick, Chair, Committee on Educational Policy, to Committee on Subject A, May, 1955.

Committee on Educational Policy to President Sproul, May 7, 1956.

Chancellor Kerr to Committee on Educational Policy, 1957.

Professor Strong, Chair, Committee on Educational Policy, to the Committee, 1957.

Professor Strong, Chair, Committee on Educational Policy, to Chancellor Kerr, May 27, 1957.

President Kerr to Committee on Educational Policy, 1963.

President Kerr to Professor V. Robinson, Chair, Committee on Educational Policy, August 20, 1965.

Professor Donald Freeman to University of California, Santa Barbara, Committee on Educational Policy, May 6, 1966.

Professor G. Pimentel, Chair, Committee on Educational Policy, to Vice President A. Taylor, May 11, 1966.

Vice President A. Taylor to University-wide Committee on Educational Policy, May 12, 1966.

Works Cited

Professor S. Markowitz to Professor G. Pimentel, Chair, Committee on Educational Policy, November 15, 1966.

Professor W. Shumaker to Professor G. Pimentel, Chair, Committee on Educational Policy, December 1, 1966.

Professor G. Pimentel, Chair, Committee on Educational Policy, to Professor S. Markowitz, December 9, 1966.

Professor B. Bridgeman, Chair, Subject A Committee, to Committee on Educational Policy, 1967.

Lecturer M. Wicksman, Supervisor, Subject A, to C. Jones, Chair, Committee on Educational Policy-Remedial Education, January 23, 1970.

Professor C. Dekker, Chair, Committee on Courses, to Professor B. O'Hehir, Chair, Committee on Remedial Education, January 1971.

Professor B. O'Hehir, Chair, Committee on Remedial Education, to C. Dekker, Chair, Committee on Courses, February 5, 1971.

Lecturer K. Newman to Dean of Letters and Science A. S. Knight, May 24, 1971.

Professor Knight to Professor O'Hehir, Chair, Committee on Educational Policy, September 13, 1971.

Professor Fawcett, Chair, Committee on Educational Policy, to Academic Senate, April 4, 1976.

President Saxon to Academic Senate, July 23, 1976.

President Saxon to Academic Senate, 1980.

Professor Davis to Subject A Committee, 1980.

Academic Senate to University-wide Committee on Educational Policy, September 1981.

Professor S. Blau, Chair, University-wide Subject A Committee, to Professor O. Johnson, Chair, Academic Council, October 1, 1981.

Professor H. Toliver, Chair, University-wide Committee on Educational Policy, to Henry Alder, Chair, Board of Admissions and Relations with Schools, October 13, 1981.

Vice President W. Fretter to chancellors, October 16, 1981.

Professor D. Bartholomae to Ad Hoc Committee to Review Subject A and SANSE, May 17, 1989.

Professor F. Crews, Chair, Committee on Preparatory and Remedial Education, to Dean of Letters and Science C. Christ, September 1, 1989.

Supervisor K. Davis to Committee on Courses of Instruction, April 17, 1991.

Lecturer S. Tollefson et al., Subject A Program, to Director K. Davis, Subject A Program, March 5, 1992.

Task Force on Improving and Increasing Writing in the Upper Division, Report, October 6, 1997.

Vice Provost V. P. J. King to Professor V. Visnawathan, Chair, Academic Planning Council, November 26, 2001.

Review of Board of Admissions and Relations with Schools, University-wide Committee on Educational Policy, University-wide Committee on Preparatory Education, Report, April 12, 2002.

Subject A Archives, 112 Wheeler Hall, UC Berkeley Campus, Sources Cited

Subject A Information Booklet, 1956.
Subject A Requirement Information Pamphlet, 1961.
Subject A Exam, 1961.

California State Archives, Sacramento, Sources Cited

President R. Sproul, Inaugural Address, October 22, 1930.
President R. Sproul, Charter Day Address, March 21, 1931.

INDEX

Connick, Robert, 82, 86

Cook, A. S., 30–31

costs, 88; contribution of conditioned students' fees, 22–24; of remedial courses, 84, 119, 120–22, 154n38, 155n39; as students' responsibility, 84, 111, 114; of Subject A instruction, 16, 111, 114, 155n39; of 13th and 14th grades, in UC *vs.* other institutions, 12, 79–80, 84

crisis management, in universities, 3

Crocker, William, 145n4, 145n7

Crowley, Sharon, 3

Cuban Missile Crisis, 101

curriculum, of high schools, 11; criticism of UC influence on, 53; Davis on need to improve, 31–32; English requirements, 121–22; university faculty certifying, 3–4, 23; university faculty supervising, 26, 43

curriculum, UC: composition in, 17, 128, 133–36; generalist, 57; influences on, 3, 62, 100; legislature criticizing, 9; under Morrill Act, 20–21

Davis, A. R., 76, 78

Davis, Horace, defending UC's standards, 9, 31–32

Davis, Kim, 118, 131–32

"The Decline in Literacy Is a Fiction, If Not a Hoax" (Ohmann), 113

Dekker, C., 108–9

demonstrations: in free speech movement, 103; at House Un-American Activities Committee hearings, 14, 99–100; against Reagan as governor, 104; at Republican National Convention, 101; students' global revolt, 152n12; against Vietnam War and Nixon, 112

departments: College Writing Programs and, 129–30; composition in, 16, 80–82, 86; expanding and upgrading, 48, 75–76; Subject A and SANSE's isolation from, 128

Deutsch, Monroe, 72

Dial. See "English in American Universities, by Professors in the English Department"

Dickson, Regent, 75

discrimination: demonstrations against, 101; against poor high schools, 106. *See also* racism

Division of Undergraduate and Interdisciplinary Studies, 134

Donovan, Richard, 115–16

Dumke, Glen, 93–94

economy, California's: agriculture in, 28–29; boom-and-bust cycles in, 3; crises in, 7, 22; decline of, 15–16, 119; education and, 52, 54, 88; effects of WWII on, 62–65; during Great Depression, 49–51, 53–54; improvement of, 9; industries in, 47, 63; influence of Southern Pacific Railroad in, 36–38; Proposition 13 and, 116, 119; relation to complaints about standards, 121; unemployment in, 148n6

economy, descriptions of, 155n10

education, 155n11; effects of tax reforms on, 116, 119–20; expected effects on economy, 54, 64, 88; legislature's studies of, 53–54, 92–93; Reagan cutting budget for, 103–4

education, higher: after WWII, 11, 64–66; Brown's support for, 92, 97; Carnegie Foundation for the Advancement of Teaching studying, 54; competition among institutions in, 78, 88–89; conditioning of underprepared students in, 21–22; crisis management in, 3; entitlement to, 2; evolution of institutions, 40, 54–55; expansion of institutions, 65–66, 68; expectations of, 66; funding for junior colleges *vs.* regional colleges, 53–54; institutions' failure to coordinate, 79–80, 93; junior colleges and, 54–55; legislature on, 22, 79, 84, 88; loyalty oaths in, 73; Master Plan for Higher Education organizing, 13–14, 21, 93–96, 113, 115, 144n2; regional colleges and, 51–54, 61, 65, 78–79, 84; remedial courses as inappropriate in, 119; role of, 47–48, 56–57, 61; as 13th and 14th grades, 12, 79–80, 84; UC's monopoly over, 51–53. *See also* graduate education; University of California

education, secondary, 7; blamed for students' poor reading and writing, 3–4, 31–32, 106–7, 121–22; discrimination against poor high schools, 106; faculty certifying curriculum of, 3–4, 23, 43; legislature criticizing UC influence on, 51–53; Subject A exam material in, 106, 114; Subject A exam scores not related to performance in, 57–58; UC relations with high schools, 21, 57, 124, 153n11;

education, secondary *(continued)*,
    university faculty supervising curriculum of, 26, 43, 60
education, training in, 94–95
Educational Opportunity Program, 109,
    117, 122, 126–28, 154n24
Educational Policies Commission, 65–66
Education Department, UC, 41, 45, 134
Eliot, Charles William, 2
elitism: accessibility *vs.*, 13, 142; UC accused
    of, 10–11, 51, 55–56
Emergency Executive Committee, 65
Engineering, College of, 42, 90–91
engineering, graduate program at San Jose
    State College, 94
English, 15–16, 59
English as a Second Language, 118, 134. *See
    also* Subject A for Non-native Speakers
    of English (SANSE)
English Department: faculty, 27, 29, 36;
    lack of importance of, 39, 41; Prose
    Improvement Project from, 81–82
English in American Universities (Payne), 25
"English in American Universities, by Professors in the English Department,"
    7–8, 25–26
enrollment, in state universities, 9
enrollment, UC, 9–10; of Asian ancestry
    students, 126; as avalanche, 41, 43; in
    College of Mechanics and Mining,
    145n11; effects of Subject A exam as
    entrance exam on, 86–87, 106–7; in
    English as a Second Language
    courses, 118; funding tied to, 48, 120;
    increasing, 22, 41, 43, 55, 103, 153n15;
    "literacy crisis" related to, 2, 57; during WWII, 64–65. *See also* admissions
Ethnic Studies Program, 107, 109
Evans, B., 77–78, 85, 136

faculty, 48, 134; administration and, 35, 39,
    72, 75; "called" to teach, 145n8; of College Writing Programs, 129–30, 132; of
    composition, 3, 29–30, 158n1; of English Department, 27, 29, 36, 39; FBI on,
    14, 98; in free speech movement, 102;
    Kerr upgrading quality of, 75–76; opposition to UC loyalty oath, 72–73;
    possessiveness over research funds,
    96–97; salaries for, 31, 39, 145n10; in
    Sproul's campaign against regional

colleges, 56; of Subject A, 15–17, 108,
    133, 139; of Subject A Office and
    SANSE, 127, 128; supervising high
    school curriculum, 23, 26, 43; suspicions of, 14, 70, 98; on underprepared
    students, 59, 67, 119, 141
Faulhaber, Charles, 125–26
Faulhaber Report, 126–27
FBI: investigating Oppenheimer, 71; investigating UC administrators, faculty, and
    students, 14, 98–100
Freeman, Donald, 154n29
free speech movement, 14, 102, 152n12
Fresno Junior College, 51
Fresno School of Agriculture, 68
Fretter, William, 89, 114, 121, 154n38
funding, UC's, 68; dependence on government research, 100; during Depression, 10, 146n5; enrollment-based, 48,
    120; influence on admission, 6–7; from
    legislature, 9, 31–32, 48, 50–51; legislature reducing, 53, 55; standards' relation to, 9, 57

Gage, Governor, 37–38
Gainsley, Director of Admissions, 115
Gann, Paul, 119
Gardner, David, 17, 131
Gardner Initiative, ending remedial
    courses, 17, 131
Gayley, Charles Mills, 145n11, 146n12; background of, 39–40; English Department
    under, 25, 39; praising UC's high standards, 25–26, 32; *Suggestions to Teachers
    of English in the Secondary Schools* by,
    3–4, 43; on underprepared students,
    7–8, 32
gender, 144n1, 146n13, 153n14; admissions
    and, 91, 106–7, 145n11; Subject A exam
    scores and, 15, 106–7
George, Henry, 28
Giannini, Regent, 72–73
GI Bill, 2, 5, 64, 147n2. *See also* veterans
Gillett, Governor, 37
Goldwater, Barry, 101
government, federal, 101; California's war
    production grants from, 62–64; Sproul
    pledging UC resources to support, 62;
    supporting higher education, 64–66,
    96–97, 112; UC research contracts
    from, 62, 100

governors, California: getting veterans higher education, 65–66; relations with UC, 10, 48, 53, 80, 92

graduate education: legislature wanting in state colleges, 68; under Master Plan for Higher Education, 94–95; other institutions' eagerness to begin, 78, 93–94, 148n8; UCB's jealous guarding of, 68, 96, 148n8

Grangers, on UC curriculum, 21

Great American Universities (Slosson), 40

Great Books lectures, 25, 39

Great Depression, 10, 49; California economy during, 53–54; higher education during, 52, 54–55; UC's emergency measures during, 55, 146n5; WWII ending, 62–63

Gwyn, William, 28

Haldeman, H. R., 112

Hart, Walter, 29–30

Harvard University, 4, 7, 139

Haynes, John Randolph, 47–48

Hearst, Phoebe Apperson, 35

Heller, Doris and Walter, 71

Herrin, William F., 37

Heyman, Ira Michael, 127

Hill, Adams Sherman, 8

Hill, Merton E., 59–60

History of English Civilization, reading on Subject A exam, 44

Hoover, J. Edgar, 14, 97–98, 100

Hopkins, Henry, 145n4

House Un-American Activities Committee, 14, 71–72, 99–100

Hudson, Arthur, 5

Hull, Glynda, 5; as College Writing Programs director, 17, 133–34; in development of College Writing Programs, 130–31

Huntington, Colis, 145n4

immigrants, 2, 122; Asian ancestry students and, 108, 118, 126–27; increasing number of students, 15–16, 103, 117

industries, 63, 65, 119

IQ, relation of Subject A exam scores to, 58

Isaac, Professor, 111–12

James, William, 25

Jarvis, Howard, 119–20

Jayne, S. R., 77

John Birch Society, 97

Johns Hopkins University, as research university model, 41

Johnson, Hiram, 10, 48

Johnson, Sabina, 109

Joint Fact-Finding Committee on Un-American Activities, 69–71

Jones, Everett, 98

Jordan, David Starr, 36, 40, 48

journalism department, Wells wanting, 38–39

junior colleges: funding for, 53–54, 85, 88; under Master Plan for Higher Education, 94–95; number of, 65, 78; pressure for upgrades of, 51, 54–55, 68, 84–85; transfer students from, 13, 76–78, 86; UC relations with, 51, 53–54, 77–79, 88

Kellogg, Martin, 39–40, 146n12

Kennedy, John F., 101

Kerr, Clark, 15n5; accusations against, 97, 103; administration of, 75, 92–93, 100, 103; on composition, 2, 82, 89, 105; effects of free speech movement on, 102, 104; Master Plan for Higher Education by, 13–14, 93–96, 144n2; ongoing struggle against state college expansion, 87–88; opposition to loyalty oath, 72; on Subject A exam as entrance exam, 87, 90; upgrading quality of faculty and departments, 75–76

King, Judson, 135–36

Knapton, E. J., 106

Knight, Goodwin, 80, 109

Knudson, Chancellor, 98

Kurtz, Benjamin, 43, 45–46

labor disputes, 37–38, 50, 66, 70, 100

labor supply, 49–50, 63, 65

Lafollette, Robert, 47–48

Lange, Alexis, 41–42

Language Acquisition Task Force, in study of remediation, 122

"The Language of Exclusion" (Rose), 3

Lawrence, Ernest O., 62

Lay, Nancy Duke, 127

legislature, California, 22, 40; criticisms of UC, 51, 53, 126; criticizing UC's standards as too high, 31, 55–56;

Index